What people are saying about …

WHAT'S YOUR SECRET?

"Aaron Stern's new book, *What's Your Secret?* is such an important message for us all, opening the way to a life that's full and free. Life in all its power is waiting for each of us as we step out of the shadows and into healing light. Let Aaron lead you on a beautiful journey to freedom as you tell the truth and let God's truth set you free."

Louie Giglio, The Passion Movement,
Passion City Church

"All of us have secrets; some of the secrets are secret sins. Not all of them get confessed. But an unconfessed secret sin is a major impediment to the health of the soul and a life of maturity in Christ. Confession has always been a major concern in the church of Jesus Christ. Aaron Stern draws on the immediacies of a richly textured pastoral practice and explores in detail what is actually involved in carrying it out. A major contribution to both Christian maturity and pastoral competence in this American culture."

Eugene H. Peterson, pastor emeritus of
spiritual theology at Regent College

"Aaron Stern is a gift to this generation and one of the most remarkable leaders I know. His writing and leadership style will challenge you to walk with integrity, strength, and grace."

Margaret Feinberg, popular speaker and author
of *Hungry for God* (www.margaretfeinberg.com)

"Aaron lays out a beautiful challenge to embrace transparency and vulnerability in every part of our lives. This book promises to help all of us walk in the light that brings freedom to every part of our souls."

Brady Boyd, senior pastor at New Life Church and author of *Fear No Evil*

"This book not only touches the heart but also gives practical wisdom to heal it. Aaron shares this ageless message in timely contemporary language that will exhilarate your Christian walk. As you follow his practical suggestions to confess, you will move from your heart to God's heart and find freedom from those issues that may have previously kept you bound."

Douglass Weiss, PhD, psychologist and author of *Get a Grip: How to Take Control of the Things That Are Controlling You*

"Aaron Stern knows what he is talking about! For over ten years, I have watched young adults find freedom through his ministry. That's why I am so thrilled to recommend *What's Your Secret?* to all. It will accelerate your journey into freedom."

David Perkins, student pastor at New Life Church and founder of Desperation Ministries

WHAT'S YOUR SECRET?

WHAT'S YOUR SECRET?

FREEDOM THROUGH CONFESSION

AARON STERN

David C Cook®
transforming lives together

WHAT'S YOUR SECRET?
Published by David C Cook
4050 Lee Vance View
Colorado Springs, CO 80918 U.S.A.

David C Cook Distribution Canada
55 Woodslee Avenue, Paris, Ontario, Canada N3L 3E5

David C Cook U.K., Kingsway Communications
Eastbourne, East Sussex BN23 6NT, England

David C Cook and the graphic circle C logo
are registered trademarks of Cook Communications Ministries.

The website addresses recommended throughout this book are offered as a
resource to you. These websites are not intended in any way to be or imply an
endorsement on the part of David C Cook, nor do we vouch for their content.

The author has changed some of the names mentioned in this book for privacy's sake.

Unless otherwise noted, all Scripture quotations are taken from the Holy
Bible, New International Version®, NIV®. Copyright © 1973, 1978, 1984 by
Biblica, Inc™. Used by permission of Zondervan. All rights reserved worldwide.
www.zondervan.com. Scripture quotations marked MSG are taken from *THE
MESSAGE*. Copyright © by Eugene H. Peterson 1993, 1994, 1995, 1996, 2000,
2001, 2002. Used by permission of NavPress Publishing Group; ESV are taken
from *The Holy Bible, English Standard Version*. Copyright © 2000; 2001 by
Crossway Bibles, a division of Good News Publishers. Used by permission. All
rights reserved; and NASB are taken from the *New American Standard Bible*, ©
Copyright 1960, 1995 by The Lockman Foundation. Used by permission.
The author has added italics to Scripture quotations for emphasis.

LCCN 2011926861
ISBN 978-1-4347-0230-2
eISBN 978-0-7814-0695-6

The Team: Alex Field, Amy Kiechlin Konyndyk,
Sarah Schultz, Jack Campbell, Karen Athen
Cover Design: JWH Graphic Arts, James Hall
Author Photo: jennarosephotography.net

Printed in the United States of America
First Edition 2011

1 2 3 4 5 6 7 8 9 10

042911

To my wife, Jossie,
for waiting for the words

CONTENTS

PART 1

COME OUT OF THE DARK

1

SECRETS CAN DESTROY YOU

What is it that no one else knows about you?

Maybe there are details about your life that, if disclosed, would result in loss or shame. A decision you wish you had never made. An event you want to forget. Maybe it's not something you did but rather *something done to you* ... a horrific violation of trust that you want obliterated from your memory. Perhaps you wrestle with tormenting feelings and thoughts that you are convinced no one will understand.

Secrets. We all have them. Human nature seems wired to withhold and tuck away the areas of our lives we deem undesirable. For many of us the best option seems to be keeping secrets out of sight and in check—and hopefully, forever forgotten.

But secrets rarely remain isolated in our hearts. Our frantic attempts to keep them at bay usually lead to an untimely unveiling.

I see it happen all the time.

FLOODGATES

I love my job. I'm a college and twentysomethings pastor, which means I get to experience a passion for life, love for adventure, and young idealism that makes for wild creativity, big risks, and lots of laughs. In the young people I pastor, I've also found a spiritual hunger that is curious, rich, and deep. I regularly find myself challenged by the intensity of their faith. Perhaps my favorite part of pastoring this demographic is that it allows me to walk with people through some of life's most critical questions, such as *Do I believe in God? What am I going to do with my life? Who will I marry?*

These young people are still figuring out what it means to be an adult and how to establish the right life patterns for the long term. In the process of doing all that, they also grapple with the past: abuse, divorce (both their parents' and their own), relationship breakups, roommate conflicts, addictions, and more. It's a pivotal time in life—a time that can be a breeding ground for keeping secrets.

This realization prompted me to do a sermon series about secrets. As a part of the series, I included an action step: I asked each person to anonymously write down a secret that no one else knew on a 1' x 1' postcard. Then I asked them to deposit their secrets into one of the baskets placed throughout the auditorium. I was hesitant, wondering if anyone would take up the challenge. Would people really write down the deepest secrets of their hearts?

When the time came, I watched in awe as the lines formed and the baskets filled up—some overflowing with little white cards. It seemed as if giving permission to share a secret had opened the floodgates. Here are just a few of the thousands of secrets collected that night and from other events, conferences, and retreats around the country:

"I CAN'T STOP HURTING MYSELF. I CAN'T STOP CUTTING."

"I HAVEN'T READ MY BIBLE IN OVER A YEAR."

"I HAD AN ABORTION LAST YEAR ... I WONDER IF I MADE THE RIGHT CHOICE."

"I'M BIPOLAR."

"MY BROTHER DIED WHEN I WAS IN THE 5TH GRADE. I HAVEN'T TOLD ANY OF MY FRIENDS THAT IT HAPPENED. KEEPING IT HIDDEN EATS ME UP EVERY DAY."

"I THINK I MIGHT BE GAY. I DIDN'T CHOOSE THIS AND I HATE IT. I'M AFRAID OF MYSELF."

"I MAKE FAKE IDs. NOT JUST ANY, BUT SOME OF THE BEST."

"I HATE MY DAD."

"I'M DATING A GOOD CHRISTIAN MAN. WE RECENTLY STARTED SLEEPING TOGETHER. IT TEARS ME UP INSIDE BUT I CAN'T TELL HIM THAT. I WANT HIM TO STOP IT."

"I AM NEVER SATISFIED WITH WHO I AM AND WHO GOD HAS CREATED ME TO BE."

"I HATE MY FRIEND FOR KILLING MY BEST
FRIEND IN A CAR ACCIDENT TWO YEARS
AGO."

"I WAS RAPED WHEN I WAS FOUR AND
THE MEMORIES OF THAT SCARE ME FROM
INTIMACY. I FEAR I WILL NEVER BE ABLE
TO BE CLOSE TO ANYONE."

"I'M IN RECOVERY FROM COCAINE AND I'VE
NEVER TOLD ANYONE ABOUT IT."

"I'M TERRIFIED THAT I WILL FIND OUT I
DON'T HAVE WHAT IT TAKES TO SUCCEED
... AT ANYTHING."

Sobering, isn't it?

Why are we willing to live with so much trapped inside? Maybe we feel that we can't stop. Or perhaps we believe that we've tried everything. We're stuck and resign ourselves to what seems to be our only option: *Put it out of sight.* Keep it in the dark. Make sure no one else knows. Suddenly we become fugitives on the run from everyone, constantly looking over our shoulders in fear that someone will find us out.

It seems safer. Cover up the unmentionables and no one gets hurt, right?

Whatever our reasons for keeping secrets, the fallout is always greater than we think. Secrets actually have the power to hurt everyone you know and love.

Things Are Not Always as They Seem

I've spent the majority of my adult life in two churches.

The pastors of both of these churches were later found to have led double lives. They preached the Bible on Sundays while having sexual trysts throughout the week. They taught on integrity while abusing church funds. They encouraged humility while living selfish lives. They taught about the light but lived in the dark. The shadows were familiar territory to them, and what happened in the shadows created monsters. And their monster secrets led to betrayal, disbelief, and truckloads of pain. Spouses, church members, employees, community leaders, colleagues, and friends—the breadth of those impacted by the carnage was huge. Nothing was left unaffected … and everything changed. And it all started with a secret.

My wife, Jossie, grew up in the "perfect" home. Her dad is a doctor who was highly respected by his colleagues and the community. She has fond memories of going to his office, playing on the hospital beds, and wearing his stethoscope. Her mom is loving and caring, and was the quintessential hostess and adoring wife. Friends and classmates regularly enjoyed her home's warmth and stable environment. The family vacationed frequently, and there was rarely a difficulty in the house. Jossie had all her needs met and most of her wants. But one day she came home from high school to find her mom sitting red faced and teary eyed across the table from her dad, who looked cold and agitated. Something was terribly wrong. When her dad said,

"I am leaving," her life and family changed forever. A mountain of questions and pain arose in the heart of a girl who had admired and looked up to her dad.

How could the perfect family fall apart? Why did this happen?

The next several months uncovered a life of secrets. Things were not as they had seemed. Secrets destroyed my wife's most valuable possession: her family. Trust was shattered and would take decades to rebuild.

Rachel was abused as a child. As a result of being violated so young, she decided she would never let anything like that happen again. She would always be in control. Food became the outward manifestation of her inward vow. She binged, then took diet pills, exercised vigilantly, and fasted for days at a time. She was in complete control and, at the same time, dwindling away. Her determination to keep her secret cost Rachel her health.

In the '90s, former president Bill Clinton was the most powerful man in the world. Despite his status as the leader of the free world, which enabled him to make things happen on a global scale with the touch of a button, he still found that he couldn't keep his secrets behind closed doors. Though he attempted to pack the details of his secret life back in the closet, it only made things worse. As a result, his legacy is remembered by the words "I did not have sexual relations with that woman." The secret he tried to keep turned into an international fiasco, costing taxpayers money, his wife her dignity, the office its respect, and a young woman her name. Though power might buy time, it can't erase the losses caused by a dangerous secret.

David, the shepherd king, had a secret. He'd been hanging out on his roof when his eye fell upon a beautiful woman named Bathsheba, bathing on her roof. He chose not to look away but rather gave himself over to temptation and desire. David invited Bathsheba to his palace, one thing led to another, and she became pregnant. Problem? Without a doubt. First of all, David wasn't married to Bathsheba, and even worse, Bathsheba was already married to Uriah, one of David's fighting men and a strong military leader. From what we can tell by reading Scripture, the guy was a superstar.

In an effort to cover his tracks, King David summoned Uriah home from the battlefield, thinking that if Uriah slept with Bathsheba, they could pass the baby off as his. However, Uriah ruined the plan when he refused to stay with his wife. His heart was with his men on the battlefield; if they couldn't enjoy their wives, than neither would he. Uriah was an honorable man. When David's plan backfired, he decided to send Uriah to the front lines where his death was inevitable. Uriah lost his life because David had a secret.

Not all secrets result in death, but all secrets can cause loss. Secrets rob us of the time and energy it takes to hide them, the grace and mercy of forgiveness and acceptance, and the growth and freedom that come from working through them. Furthermore, it is a lie to think that we can keep our secrets from spinning out of control and hurting others. As long as they are kept, secrets never shrink, they never go away, and they never lead to life.

CONSEQUENCES

Unfortunately stories like these seem to be the norm. The uncovering of secrets rarely shocks us anymore. A CEO steals from the company coffers, a pastor betrays the trust of a congregation, or a politician attempts an illegal activity. Secrets are everywhere.

Take marriage, for example. Marriage is *the* most intimate relationship experienced by humanity. Yet research reveals that even in that close-knit union, secrets fester.

One survey found that about 40 percent of married Americans admit keeping a secret from their spouses. The most common secret is how much money they spend.

A different study broke it down further and estimated that approximately 42 percent of men and 36 percent of women admit keeping something from their mates. Boomers, big-wage earners, and those married a long time are the most likely to have secrets.

Regarding infidelity, about 12 percent of men and 7 percent of women will have an affair at some point in marriage.[1]

Sadly most of us have heard, been party to, or walked alongside someone who fits into these statistics. A husband hides his

pornography addiction, a wife conceals her impulsive spending habits on an unknown credit card, or friends lie to friends.

(**"I CAN'T STAND MYSELF. I HATE MY MOM BECAUSE I SEE MYSELF IN HER."**)

We may think that we are keeping a secret, but the truth is that the secret is actually keeping us. What we thought we controlled, slowly and subtly grows.

It's hard to imagine a marriage or a close friendship deepening in intimacy if a piece of the person's heart is walled up, available to no one. Secrets leave parts of us unavailable, and as a result, the emotional fallout is massive. Unhealthy patterns are cultivated, and growth is stunted by the drive to cover up lies. Feelings become shuttered, dreams are denied, and vision is blurred.

Even our best efforts to hide or deny the problem can't unburden our thoughts. We become emotionally muted, dominated by shame, depression, anxiety, fear, insecurity, and heaviness. In an effort to self-protect, we avoid and eventually lose the friendships and community we need the most.

Eventually the secrets burst out. It's like stepping on a toothpaste tube with the cap on. The tube responds to the pressure and bursts at its weakest point, creating a big mess in the process.

There is scientific evidence that, over time, even our physical health is compromised by the emotional burden of holding on to a secret. In his book *Deadly Emotions: Understand the Mind-Body-Spirit*

Connection That Can Heal or Destroy You, author Don Colbert shows the symptoms and potentially deadly effects of holding things in. Here are just a few:

- Anger and hostility are linked to hypertension and coronary artery disease.
- Resentment, bitterness, unforgiveness, and self-hatred are connected to autoimmune disorders, rheumatoid arthritis, lupus, and multiple sclerosis.
- Anxiety is tied to irritable-bowel syndrome, panic attacks, mitral-valve prolapse, and heart palpitations.
- Those who live under guilt and shame are more likely to have issues with chronic depression.[2]

Quite a grim picture, isn't it? However, the greatest toll our secret-keeping takes is on our spiritual lives. Our desire to hide translates into distance from God. After all, who would choose to put themselves in a relationship with a God who knows everything if our highest motivation is to protect a secret?

("I CAN'T FIND GRACE FOR MY DAD. HE EMBARRASSES ME AND I'M ANGRY EVERY TIME HE FAILS.")

Anytime we encounter a spiritual problem, it can be helpful to look at our heritage ... *as in our biblical heritage.* Besides, this whole business began with Adam and Eve and the talking-snake, fruit-eating incident that changed everything. How did they respond? Yep, you guessed it. When they realized that they had messed up and disobeyed God, they tried to keep it a secret. Their shame and sudden awareness of both their physical and spiritual nakedness drove them—literally—into the bushes. It turns out this tendency of ours to run away from God goes all the way back to the beginning.

(**"I AM ARROGANT AND NOT COMPASSIONATE. THE HATE IN ME EATS AWAY AT MY HEART."**)

However, the questions may remain in our heads and hearts: *So what's the big deal? If no one else knows, the only person my secret hurts is me, right?* Perhaps. But that is reason enough.

God longs for us to walk intimately with Him, to be free to engage life and relationships without the stain of shame, hurt, and regret. And there is also the uncomfortable reality that secrets aren't stagnant. They grow—and the dark recesses of our hearts provide fertile soil.

The Desert Fathers were a community of monks who lived in the Egyptian desert beginning in the third century. They had a collection of sayings that reinforce the weighty power of things hidden. One of those reads, "The more a person conceals his thoughts, the more they multiply and gain strength. If you hide things, they have great power over you."

Samuel Johnson, a British author in the 1700s, wisely said, "Where secrecy or mystery begins, vice or roguery is not far off."

BARNACLES

On a recent family vacation to California, my family and I visited the Monterey Bay Aquarium. Since I'm from the landlocked state of Colorado, the trip fascinated me. I saw octopuses and sharks and even some sea creatures I never knew existed! One of the things I found most interesting were the bits of information that we learned on the guided tours, videos, or signs placed near exhibits. My favorite piece of information was about barnacles (and how can you not love saying the word *barnacle?*).

Barnacles attach themselves to things like whales, ships, and even rocks, living out their lives stuck to the undersides of other objects. Barnacles even make whales slower in the water, inhibiting their ability to swim smoothly.

(**"I STRUGGLE WITH LUST AND MASTURBATION."**)

Secrets are like barnacles: They attach themselves to us and slow us down as we travel through life. Keeping secrets is not just a matter of speed but of us being fully alive. The more secrets we keep and the longer we keep them, the less alive … the less human we become. Secrets cause us to live at a distance from God and others, and the fullness of who we are—the good, bad, and ugly—cannot fully engage in life.

A secret in its simplest form is merely information. However, it is keeping this information hidden that gives control to the enemy.

The enemy of our souls uses secrets to destroy us from the inside out. Secrets of any kind can lead to the physical, emotional, and spiritual consequences all too familiar in our society. Sins of commission or omission, family secrets, secret thoughts, and even feelings can quickly attach to shame, fear, lack of value, and a myriad of other barnacle-like emotions, slowing us down and causing loss.

So now what?

At this point, you may be thinking, *Wow. You certainly have painted a bleak picture. I understand that secrets of any kind are bad, but living without secrets sounds impossible. Where would I start? What would it look like to have a life without secrets? How can I quit sabotaging my relationships with God and others? Is it possible?*

Yes. I watch it every day in the lives of the people I pastor. We can also see it played out in Scripture. Galatians 5:1 says, "It is for freedom that Christ has set us free. Stand firm, then, and do not let yourselves be burdened again by a yoke of slavery." Burden, bondage, and fear aren't God's way. Freedom is possible and it is God's idea, not just in eternity but today.

God gave us a way to live where secrets don't have to grow and then explode when we least expect it. We don't have to live scared for the next twenty years, wondering if our hidden thoughts, behaviors, and pain will find a way out. Remember Adam and Eve? God came looking for them. And He is looking for you.

So where do we start?

The path to freedom begins with an act: *confession.*

REFLECTION

/// Do you have a secret?

/// In what ways have you experienced the consequences of
someone else's secret?

/// How do you think you would feel if you didn't keep any
secrets?

2

CONFESS TO GOD

My wife doesn't like messes. In fact, she loves wiping off countertops and dusting. Over the last fifteen years of marriage, we have argued many times over how and when to clean things.

One moment stands out clearly in my mind. We were in a rush to make it to a party with friends. Punctuality has never been one of our strong suits, but we really do try. My hair was in place, my teeth brushed, and I was dressed for the occasion, and it seemed like Jossie was ready too. I had my jacket on and keys in hand when I called out, "Let's go," to which her response was, "Just a minute."

"What are you doing?" I asked.

"Cleaning the bathroom!"

Extremely perplexed, I made my way toward the smell of surface and glass cleaner. "What do you mean you're cleaning the bathroom? Isn't that something you could do another time? We're late and need to go. Why now?"

"Well, I just want to make sure that the house is clean *just in case* someone comes over after the party."

I saw the situation differently in two key ways. First, I didn't think the bathroom was dirty (I have since learned that my man eyes only see an object as dirty when something starts to visibly grow on it). Second, none of our guests would carefully inspect the shower walls.

Our little marital conflict about the bathroom reflects some basic tendencies we all have. Consider the less tangible but more influential realm of our thoughts, emotions, dreams, sins, disappointments, and decisions. Most of us don't want anyone to know about our internal messes, nor allow them to be seen. We would much rather clean things up first and eliminate the remnants of grossness, insecurity, or emotional unrest.

It's not unusual for us to try this tactic with God; we try to clean ourselves up before we come to Him. We want to present a life that is in order and free of the things that would turn Him off. After all, God doesn't like dirt, right? But by trying to tidy ourselves up, we think we're dealing with the most important issue at hand and we may even pat ourselves on the back for our diligent efforts to make ourselves presentable. In reality though, we're totally missing the point. It's like putting a suit and tie on a monkey: No matter how sharp the suit looks, it's still a pick-things-out-of-its-friend's-hair-and-eat-it primate that's wearing it. Window dressing doesn't change the insides.

("I DON'T BELIEVE ANYONE LOVES ME, NOT EVEN GOD.")

HEROES?

In a refreshing and, at times, uncomfortable manner, Scripture makes it clear that the human beings in whom God works are incredibly flawed. These men and women of God whom we sometimes see as heroes were never intended for a pedestal. *Far from it.* Consider these life summaries of our scriptural "giants":

Moses killed a guy and spent years traipsing around a desert trying to forget. His response to God asking him to assume a key leadership role in the kingdom was fearful and insecure and followed by a blunt "Find someone else to do it, God!" This is not exactly the picture of Israel's fearless deliverer!

(**"I HAVE STOLEN THOUSANDS OF DOLLARS WORTH OF MOVIES, MUSIC, AND MEDIA."**)

Rahab was a prostitute who demonstrated quick wits and fearless leadership when she hid Israelite spies to save her family. Yes, that's right—a prostitute! Yet we find her listed in the lineage of Jesus (Matt. 1:5).

Abraham, the father of many nations and the patriarch of our faith, doubted God's promise for a son and took things into his own hands. Given his wife, Sarah's, old age, he slept with his maidservant to help God out. Sarah fared little better—she actually laughed at God when He promised her a son.

Peter experienced numerous ups and downs with Jesus. One minute he was the rock upon which Jesus would build the church,

the next he was a tool of Satan. Ultimately Peter was humiliated
by his inability to stand faithful during Jesus' trial and crucifixion.

And Paul seemed to pull the words right out of our hearts
when he wrote about his own struggle: "I do not understand what
I do. For what I want to do I do not do, but what I hate I do....
For I have the desire to do what is good, but I cannot carry it out"
(Rom. 7:15, 18).

These real-life stories do not attempt to hide or minimize the
brokenness of humanity or life's messiness. These are the people
God works the most with—those least qualified and full of problems, insecurities, and sin. If God's goal was to use perfect people
or even people who seemed perfect, He would've chosen to accom-
plish His work a little differently ... or leave the fallible humans out
of the equation altogether. God's plan and work are best portrayed
in the messes of our lives. *We've missed the point by thinking we need
to have it all together.*

("I LIE TO MY ACCOUNTABILITY PARTNER
ABOUT MY MASTURBATION AND LUST
HABIT.")

YOU DID WHAT?

So if God knowingly and willingly enters our brokenness, how
should we respond?

With *confession*—living honestly before God and making
sure that the contents of our hearts match what we share with

Him. For many of us, that's easier said than done. Our natural tendency shies away from true openness. In fact, I am amazed at the thoughts that go through our minds: *God can't love me unless I figure this out. God won't give me another chance—I've exhausted His do-over capacity.* And my all-time favorite: *What is God going to think?*

As if He doesn't know already!

Do we think He is going to be surprised? That somehow when we spill the beans, God will react to our sin with an "Oh My Self!" and sit down to absorb the shock? For better or for worse, He already knows. The Bible tells us that He knows everything about us, right down to the number of hairs on our heads.

Consider Psalm 139:1–8:

> O LORD, you have searched me
>   and you know me.
> You know when I sit and when I rise;
>   you perceive my thoughts from afar.
> You discern my going out and my lying down;
>   you are familiar with all my ways.
> Before a word is on my tongue
>   you know it completely, O LORD.
> You hem me in—behind and before;
>   you have laid your hand upon me.
> Such knowledge is too wonderful for me,
>   too lofty for me to attain.
> Where can I go from your Spirit?
>   Where can I flee from your presence?

If I go up to the heavens, you are there;

if I make my bed in the depths, you are there.

There is no getting away from God. No escaping His knowledge. He knows what you do before you do it. He knows what you think. He saw what happened to you and He knew what was in your heart *before* it became a secret. To hide from God is like hiding Christmas gifts from a twelve-year-old boy (sorry, Mom and Dad). It's pointless!

Maybe you're already asking yourself this question: *If God already knows, then what's the benefit of spilling the beans? Doesn't His mind-reading ability negate the need for confession?* No. Confession is not for God; it's for us. Confessing our secrets to God takes the sin and shame out of our hands. We are not capable of getting rid of our own messes—that process belongs to the Lord.

"If we confess our sins, he is faithful and just and will forgive us our sins and purify us from all unrighteousness" (1 John 1:9).

Our part? *Confession.* His part? *Forgiveness.*

> "I WAS ASSAULTED WHEN I WAS 9. I LOST THAT INNOCENCE AND CAN NEVER GET IT BACK."

FEELINGS

In my years as a pastor I have regularly heard people say "There isn't any condemnation in Christ" in response to the sadness and pain they feel when they are encouraged to bring the dark and sinful areas of their hearts into the light before God. This is a massive misunderstanding of the meaning of this passage as well as what their feelings mean. The best way to clarify this is to understand the difference between condemnation and conviction.

Condemnation comes from the enemy, is all about guilt, and asks the question, *What good are you?* or, *How could you?* The end goal of condemnation is to draw you *away* from God.

Conviction comes from the Holy Spirit, is all about redemption, and simply asks the question, *What did you do?* This is the same question that God asked Adam and Eve in the garden after they had sinned (Gen. 3). The end goal of conviction is to draw you back *to* God.

("I LOVE PORN."   )

Conviction also leads you to confession and repentance of specific and identifiable sins and secrets. Conviction may not always feel good, but the purpose goes beyond our personal comfort. Restoration of relationships is the driving force behind conviction. Don't resist the conviction of the Holy Spirit only because you feel bad; it's the very thing that leads to confession.

RAW AND REAL

Confession also challenges us to take a real hard look at our hearts. We are often tempted to simply give an excuse or to offer God a justification or explanation of our motives and intent. Our difficult circumstances, personality flaws, poor upbringing, weak education, or misfortunes can all become excuses we use to minimize the importance of the sin we're confessing. Such caveats are not true confessions though. Eugene Peterson, author of *The Message* Bible, says it this way: "No excuses, no rationalizations, no denial, no New Year's resolutions, only 'I will confess....'"[3]

Noelle, one of my former staff members, is a naturally gifted counselor and pastor. She meets with young women constantly, providing spiritual direction and God's perspective on the issues in their lives.

(**"I HAVE STOLEN FROM EVERY EMPLOYER I'VE EVER HAD."**)

After hearing one girl's story of being trapped in a cycle of cutting and extreme loneliness, Noelle asked her to close their time together in prayer. The girl refused. Noelle was taken aback and asked what was behind her resistance. Several possible answers floated through her head: *She's shy and doesn't like praying in front of others. She is unsure of what to say. She is afraid of the emotions that may arise after talking about such a sensitive issue.*

The answer was not what Noelle expected:

"I DON'T WANT TO PRAY ALOUD BECAUSE IF I DO, IT WILL MAKE IT REAL."

By refusing to acknowledge her pain aloud in prayer, she kept it in the realm of theory. If she confessed her pain to God aloud, it would become a reality that she would be forced to face. She would have to forgive others, she would have to repent, and she would have to change direction. Confession to God was the linchpin. It would open the floodgates of reality, responsibility, and obedience.

> "I DIDN'T STOP HIM BECAUSE EVEN THOUGH I KNEW HE WAS DRUNK AND HAD PLENTY OF OTHER GIRLS TO FOOL AROUND WITH ... I JUST WANTED TO FEEL WANTED BY SOMEONE."

Remember David? Our roof-perched, Peeping Tom, sleeping-with-the-wife-of-his-army-commander, director-of-the-*Godfather*-like killing-of-her-husband king? *That guy?* Well, after all the mess he created, David tried to keep his sin a secret. He thought he had gotten away with murder (literally!) and was home free. But God knew and wasn't going to let the secret stay hidden. Enter the prophet Nathan. God sent him to David to expose his secret. After David was confronted with his sin, he confessed to God:

> Have mercy on me, O God,
>   according to your unfailing love;
> according to your great compassion
>   blot out my transgressions.
> Wash away all my iniquity
>   and cleanse me from my sin.

> For I know my transgressions,
>> and my sin is always before me.
> Against you, you only, have I sinned
>> and done what is evil in your sight,
> so that you are proved right when you speak
>> and justified when you judge.
> Surely I was sinful at birth,
>> sinful from the time my mother conceived me.
>> (Ps. 51:1–5)

Notice David's blunt honesty and decision not to sugarcoat the truth. He doesn't deny, deflect, minimize, or rationalize. David lets it all hang out. He calls himself sinful and evil and admits his inability to fix the problem. David's honest confession is a model for us.

When we're caught doing something wrong, most of us will quickly promise not to do it again rather than repent for what we've already done. Chastened by discovery rather than conviction, we buckle down and determine to work harder.

> "I will try my hardest to not cut myself again to relieve pain."
> "I will not visit that pornography site ever again."
> "I promise not to sleep with my boyfriend until we are married."

Our resolve serves us well initially, but it doesn't last long. Our human strength is limited, so nice words and good intentions can carry us only so far. After awhile, internal wrestling gets the best of us and we fall into our secret behaviors once more.

Confession like David's pulls us out of the puny, self-deceiving contrivances we attempt in order to manage sin on our own. It requires us to say honestly, "I am a cutter and need help with my emotional pain," "I am a sex addict," or, "I am afraid my boyfriend will leave if I don't sleep with him."

Painful? Yes. Hopeful? Absolutely.

(**"I'M ALWAYS SAD, BUT I SMILE MORE THAN ANYONE I KNOW."**)

Neil Anderson wrote that unless people are emotionally honest their chances of resolving conflicts and being set free from the past are slim. You cannot be right with God and not be real emotionally.[4]

Without confession, we are unable to acquire the necessary tools to walk out of darkness. Confession teaches humility, submission, and openness. This practice demands that we learn to receive what we so desperately need: *forgiveness*. It is the first step that makes all other steps possible. David realized the freedom he experienced from sharing his darkest secrets with God.

> When I kept silent about my sin, my body wasted
>   away
>   Through my groaning all day long.

For day and night Your hand was heavy upon me;
  My vitality was drained away as with the fever heat
  of summer. Selah.
I acknowledged my sin to You,
  And my iniquity I did not hide;
  I said, "I will confess my transgressions to the
  LORD";
  And You forgave the guilt of my sin. Selah.
  (Ps. 32:3–5 NASB)

David's honesty allowed him to experience God's love in a fresh way. "Many are the sorrows of the wicked, but he who trusts in the LORD, lovingkindness shall surround him" (Ps. 32:10 NASB).

(**"I FEAR THAT IF I CRY I BECOME WEAKER."**)

IT'S NOT OVER

I wonder if past experiences with pharisaical churches and "religious leaders" have colored our views of what God will do if we tell Him what's in our hearts? The question of "What will God think?" moves quickly to "If I tell Him, how will He respond?" Will He kick me to the curb? Am I damaged goods, tainted for future use in the kingdom? Will His disappointment be too much to bear?

Our backward thinking leads us to believe that God takes secret pleasure in being angry. Confession introduces us to what Eugene Peterson described as "the vast world of forgiveness, encompassed with God's deliverance and steadfast love."[5]

Take a look at this:

> Who is a God like you,
>> who pardons sin and forgives the transgression
>> of the remnant of his inheritance?
> You do not stay angry forever
>> but delight to show mercy.
> You will again have compassion on us;
>> you will tread our sins underfoot
>> and hurl all our iniquities into the depths of the
>> sea. (Mic. 7:18–19)

Amazing change of perspective, isn't it? How about this one:

> He does not treat us as our sins deserve
>> or repay us according to our iniquities.
> For as high as the heavens are above the earth,
>> so great is his love for those who fear him;
> as far as the east is from the west,
>> so far has he removed our transgressions from us.
>> (Ps. 103:10–12)

God isn't going to hold your confessions over your head. He wants to see you whole. So tap into His mercy, which is like rain in the desert, or fresh water to a parched soul. His desire is that we drink fully and drink freely. It may not be easy, but easy has never been the stipulation for obedience. Take the big step. Confess to God, and He will forgive.

Just as we can't clean ourselves up before we go to God (though we sure do try), the act of confession to God does not make the mess go away either. Forgiveness and mess removal are not synonymous. In confession to God we freely receive forgiveness from Him and experience the light as He breaks into the dark recesses of our hearts. But forgiveness is not a spiritual power washer—the mess is still there.

If that step was all that was required, then this would be a short book. Confession to God is only the beginning.

REFLECTION

/// Does it help you to know that the Bible is full of imperfect people?

If so, why?

/// In what ways do you try to hide the mess of your life from God?

/// Are you afraid to confess openly and honestly to God?

If so, what are you afraid of?

3

CONFESS TO OTHERS

Have you ever gone to church and watched the same people kneel and pray at the altar up front after every service? As a pastor I see it all the time. You know what is often happening there? Are people dedicating their lives to God? Definitely. Are people humbling their hearts before their loving Father? Absolutely. Rededication? Yes, though sometimes I call it a rededication of a rededication of a rededication. Often people are confessing the same sin to God over and over again. Yes, they receive forgiveness each time, but there is a deeper issue at stake. *Why aren't they getting over it?* That is the million-dollar question. But wait a second. Isn't confession the key?

Confession is the key, but it's only the beginning. James 5:16 says, "Therefore confess your sins to each other and pray for each other so that you may be healed. The prayer of a righteous man is powerful and effective."

Confessing to God provides forgiveness, while confessing to someone else provides healing. Lots of people have found forgiveness, but they need healing to overcome and move beyond their secrets.

But doesn't healing come from Jesus? Isn't confession just about me getting right with God? Why is confession to another person necessary? Can't forgiveness and healing come in the same package? It seems like that would be much easier. If Jesus is the healer, why do I need to tell someone else my secret?

Let's look at the context of James 5:16 to get a better grasp on what God is encouraging us to do here. James 5:14–15 says, "Is any one of you sick? He should call the elders of the church to pray over him and anoint him with oil in the name of the Lord. And the prayer offered in faith will make the sick person well; the Lord will raise him up. If he has sinned, he will be forgiven."

Are the elders the ones who heal? Can you experience healing by praying for yourself? Should you pray to the elders, or should you pray to Jesus?

James painted the picture of Jesus as a healer who works *through* the community of faith.

James said we need others.

Did James write "the two steps to healing"? No. He encouraged us as believers to be healed by the body of Christ, to lay out our brokenness and pain not simply before God in the privacy of our hearts, but also before those around us.

This is going to require soul-searching courage. Not only the courage to face it yourself but also the courage to show someone else. By keeping the secrets of our hearts locked behind closed doors, we think we can avoid what lurks in the depths. Maybe we try to avoid it because we're scared that we won't be able to bear the pain or shame of its revelation. Maybe we want to avoid it because we're concerned about what people will think. Our avoidance can even be so powerful that we don't see ourselves as we really are, living out of what we *wish* we were instead. As appealing as this might sound, it will only give greater control to the very thing we are trying to avoid.

If we keep our secrets to ourselves long enough, Frederick Buechner says "we run the risk of losing track of who we truly and fully are and little by little we will come to accept instead the highly edited version which we put forth in hope that the world will find it more acceptable than the real thing."[6]

While part of us might be terrified of admitting our secrets *to ourselves,* let alone sharing them with someone else, within all of us there's an even deeper desire to be truly known.

(**"I HAD SEX AT THE AGE OF 12."**   )

ANONYMITY

In 2004, Frank Warren, a businessman from Maryland, decided to find out what secrets people held on to and had never told anyone. He printed three thousand self-addressed postcards with an invitation to mail him an anonymous personal secret. Artistic expression was encouraged.

He then placed these cards in public places where people would find them and respond—Starbucks tables, in the pages of books at the library, benches in museums, etc. At first, a few cards made their way back to his address. After four years he'd received over three hundred thousand postcards. Some of the secrets were on the cards he'd created, while many more came back on homemade postcards. People wanted to tell their darkest secrets to a guy they didn't know and would probably never meet. It was as if the pressure that had built up over time had finally been given an outlet. Warren continues to get one to two hundred postcards a day! So many have come in that he published compilations of some of the secrets in a series called PostSecret.

One of my all-time favorite secrets was sent to Warren on the sleeve of a Starbucks cup, reading, "I give decaf to customers who are rude to me!"[7] As difficult as it sometimes may be without caffeine in my system, I am now extra careful to treat my Starbucks barista with excessive care, respect, and gratitude!

The PostSecret projects might tap into our voyeuristic tendencies, and sending in a postcard may make us feel better knowing that our secrets are known by *someone*. But while this idea is a good one, it is far from complete.

James didn't tell us to confess our sins anonymously via the US Postal Service; rather his encouragement was to confess to a living, breathing person. It is difficult to pray for "Anonymous" and impossible to respond. The ministry of Jesus was always personal and never anonymous. James carried the way of Jesus into confession. Confession needs to be personal … so people we know can personally pray with and for us.

To confess anonymously without involving others, without engaging the community of God, is a good exercise in navel gazing. It's interesting but ultimately unproductive. It would be nice if anonymous confession was all it took. It might be a baby step, but it is definitely not the last step. God has something bigger in mind. Something that requires giving up on the feeling of security by holding things in. Something that requires letting your walls down and showing the darkness in your heart to someone else. I love James 5:16 in *The Message*: "Make this your common practice: Confess your sins to each other and pray for each other so that you can live together whole and healed." God's reason for confession to another human being is about wholeness of heart and wholeness of relationship.

(**"I SLEPT WITH MY BOYFRIEND, GOT PREGNANT, AND HAD A MISCARRIAGE."**)

In the beautifully honest autobiography of Frederick Buechner, *Telling Secrets,* he muses, "I not only have my secrets, I am my secrets. And you are your secrets. Our secrets are human secrets, and our trusting each other enough to share them with each other has much to do with the secret of what it is to be human."[8]

Speaking your secret aloud to another person makes it real. All of a sudden it's out there. Suddenly your secret isn't a theory, a bad dream, or just an idea. And making your secret real forces you to face it. *Now someone else knows.* You are completely exposed, vulnerable, and naked.

But vulnerability alone is not the point. Vulnerability is a launching pad, the start of a journey to something better—much better.

In his book *Seven: The Deadly Sins and the Beatitudes*, author Jeff Cook wrote, "Every story about a fall from grace is first a story about privacy. Every story about dramatic restoration of character is first a story of exposure."[9]

This idea of confession was a good idea long before James, the brother of Jesus, penned his letter around AD 45 (some scholars put the date as late as AD 50). Proverbs 28:13 says, "You can't whitewash your sins and get by with it; you find mercy by admitting and leaving them" (MSG).

So how can we confess? In *The Great Gatsby*, the wonderful novel by F. Scott Fitzgerald, Nick Carraway, the narrator, finds himself the recipient of many a secret and says at one point, "The intimate revelations of young men, or at least the terms in which they express them, are usually plagiaristic and marred by obvious suppressions."[10] The point is a good one. True confession doesn't involve copying what we've heard others say or leaving out parts that are just a bit too vulnerable.

(**"I HAVE AT LEAST ONE THOUGHT OF DYING EVERY DAY."**)

To confess to others requires the same brutal honesty required when confessing to God. Just as David laid out his confession plain and clear to God in Psalm 51, we also must be straightforward and honest with those closest to us.

Thomas Brooks, the Puritan sea chaplain and London preacher, once said, "An implicit confession is almost as bad as an implicit faith; wicked men commonly confess their sins by wholesale. We are all sinners; but the true penitent confesses his sins by retail."[11]

Don't take the easy road of denial, deflection, minimization, or rationalization. Put it all out there, details and all. Don't spin it.

UNCONFESSION

Because of the age and life stage of those I pastor, I perform weddings on a regular basis. I've even done two in one day! Fortunately one of my favorite things about my job is officiating all these weddings. I love the flowers, the tuxedos, the beautiful dresses, the fathers walking their daughters down the aisles, the music … I love it all. I consider it a privilege to be a part of such special and sacred events. Before the vows, the rings, and the kisses, I do a lot of premarital counseling.

In the first session I always ask the couple to tell me about their physical relationship. One couple in particular told me, "Things are good. We have boundaries and have committed to not having sex until we are married." This sounded good, but I'd been doing this long enough to know that this kind of answer wasn't going to cut it. I needed some details. So I started to dig, and after about fifteen more minutes of questioning, I found that they had slept together several months prior and their boundaries were loose at best … *oh, and now they were living together.* Had I left their initial answer alone, I think they would have been relieved and felt satisfied with their level of disclosure. Now the truth was out, but this was hardly a confession.

Afterward they said they felt lighter not carrying around the weight of their secret. They were glad to get the secret out in the open, *all of it.*

Our tendency is to withhold information so we don't look quite so bad. We have an image to uphold and a reputation to maintain. So we try to keep our image intact and still let people into our lives. That's a win-win, right? *Wrong.* This is what we so often sound like:

> "We kinda messed up a bit one time." (minimization)
> "My sister was extremely mean to me, and I didn't respond very well." (rationalization)
> "I really am loving and caring. I really have a big heart for people and always mean to be kind, but one time I accidentally hurt my friend." (deflection)

By keeping the details in the dark, our goal is to make people think it really isn't a big deal. However, when we put it all out there, our honesty helps bring a weight to the situation. Our honesty gives specificity to those praying for us and tangibility to true account-ability. The details are huge. We should sound more like this:

> "We have had oral sex three times in the last month" (leave the explanation for later).
> "I yelled at my sister and told her that I hated her."
> "I told lies about my friend."

(**"I LUST AFTER MY FRIEND'S WIFE."**)

The complete truth may be embarrassing, but it is in our embarrassment that God is at work. When the details are laid out, the results are rich. Check out this story:

> "FOR THE LAST FEW MONTHS I HAD BEEN FEELING LIKE SOMETHING WAS HOLDING ME BACK FROM THE HIGHEST AND BEST THAT GOD HAS FOR MY LIFE. AFTER HEARING YOUR TALK ON SECRETS, MY WIFE AND I TOLD EACH OTHER EVERY SECRET WE EVER HAD AND IT HAS TRANSFORMED OUR RELATIONSHIP WITH EACH OTHER AND GOD TO NEW LEVELS OF SWEETNESS. EVEN SECRETS WE DIDN'T THINK MATTERED HAVE DRAWN US CLOSER."

When there is openness and honesty in our relationships, the intimacy for which God designed us actually grows.

A Culture of Confession

One time at theMILL, the college/twentysomethings ministry at the church where I pastor, I had a conversation with a guy who really got under my skin. At one point in the conversation he accused me of not caring for someone whom I cared for deeply. In my frustration I let out an expletive in my response to his statement.

Immediately I wanted to go back in time and pull the cuss word back into my mouth. I was shocked at myself. I never talk like that! I soon found myself apologizing for my lack of restraint. A couple hours later I had a staff meeting and quickly brought up the incident and my response with my coworkers. My first instinct was to keep the incident hidden, but I want to live out in the open, lead by example, and create a culture of sharing our lives with one another. I want vulnerability to be the norm and authenticity to be the currency of deep relationships.

On another occasion, I publicly repented to theMILL for a video I had shown the week before that was meant to be a joke but in the end didn't reflect Jesus or the heart of our ministry.

It's easy for us to slide past these types of faux pas without saying a peep, but when we show our willingness to confess, it says something about the awareness of our brokenness and gives permission to blow it and still be loved.

I take my role as a dad to my four boys very seriously. I try to teach them constantly, both directly and indirectly. One thing I want them to do quickly and with regularity is to confess and repent for their sins.

(**"I TAKE PAIN PILLS TO HAVE ENERGY AND GET THROUGH THE DAY."**)

Job 1:1 says this: "Job was a man who lived in Uz. He was honest inside and out, a man of his word, who was totally devoted to God and hated evil with a passion" (MSG). Job didn't allow darkness to build in his heart. He took the need for bringing things out of the shadows so seriously that he would repent on his kids' behalf for sins they might have committed (Job 1:5).

I want to be like Job: quick to examine my heart and then to bring it to God and others. My wife and I confess and repent to our kids if we've treated them poorly. When our boys blow it, we have them confess to God and others very specifically as they ask for forgiveness. One of my boys might say:

> "[INSERT ONE OF HIS BROTHERS' NAMES HERE], I'M SORRY FOR HITTING YOU IN THE FACE AND NOT TREATING YOU KINDLY. WILL YOU FORGIVE ME?"

I want confession to be a part of who they are. Not something they shy away from, but something that is natural and organic to who they are as people.

After receiving the hundreds of anonymous secrets at theMILL, I picked out a few to read each week. I left out any details that would reveal the author. Here's one I read:

> "I'M 20 YEARS OLD, AND I'VE NEVER BEEN IN A RELATIONSHIP. I TELL PEOPLE THAT IT'S BECAUSE I'M WAITING, BUT I KNOW THAT IN REALITY I'M JUST TERRIFIED OF PUTTING MY HEART ON THE LINE. I DON'T SEE HOW I COULD SUCCEED IN A RELATIONSHIP SINCE I'M SO SCARED OF THE COMMITMENT. THE DESIRE FOR THAT CLOSENESS WITH A WOMAN BURNS IN ME, BUT THE FEAR THAT I AM NOT MAN ENOUGH FOR THAT KIND OF RELATIONSHIP OVERWHELMS ME."

The next day I got this email:

My name is Michael and I stuck my card with my little secret on it into the box up front. This past Friday, as you were reading a few off from the stage, I was quite surprised (and a little shocked/nervous) when I heard mine being read. As I was sitting there surrounded by friends listening to my card being read in front of the whole auditorium, I can't deny that the first thing that went through my mind was "What in the world?! That was a secret!"

By the time theMILL was over and I was in the car riding home with one of my friends, I reached the point where I could admit to my buddy that my card was read in front of everyone. From there the changes have been interesting. Just by talking to someone, I've realized how small and almost silly my "secret" fears are. And let me tell you, having your secret told to hundreds and hundreds of people sure makes it easier to talk to close friends about!

I'm not sure which has had more of an effect on me: having my secret "fears" made known, or realizing how little of a grip those fears should have on my life. After taking a big step back and looking at where I am in life, I can see that there's absolutely no reason that I should let myself be held back by things such as the fear of failure, the fear of rejection, and the many other fears that seem to come with relationships. Also, ironically enough, by dropping my own guard a little bit, I've begun to notice how many people around me are working through exactly the same types of feelings. I know that I won't be able to just instantly shake off all the

*aftereffects of years of trying to keep my relationship fears hidden, but it's a
big relief simply to have finally addressed them!*

A few months later I got this email update from Michael:

*After I realized that that fear was not worthy of being a secret,
I started doing a ton of growing and have turned into much more
of a man. In fact, I finally got up the courage to ask out the girl who
had been the source of all my "fear of relationship" versus "wanting to
date" frustration. We've been very happily dating for the past couple of
months. In fact, your talk on secrets came up once while she and I were
talking. Ironically, she had wanted really badly to meet the guy who
wrote the card about being afraid of relationships and be his friend so
that he'd know that girls were nothing to be afraid of. Ha ha, I guess
she got her wish! We were friends before that, but now we're much
closer. It's almost funny how God works sometimes.*

As if this story couldn't get any better, Michael and Kristin are
now married and expecting a baby boy (they emailed me recently
saying they were looking forward to teaching him not to be afraid
of relationships). How's that for a good reason to confess your
secrets?

You might be thinking that these secrets are "easy." Maybe
you're thinking, *Aaron, if you knew my secret, you would see how
difficult it really is.* For you, even the thought of telling someone
sends chills down your spine. Consider this email I received from
a girl named Hillary four months after I talked about secrets at
theMILL.

I have a secret, and I have been struggling with it for two years now. It amazes me when I think that it's been two years and it's still a big struggle in my life. And I know now that I can't keep on living my life like this, it has to stop. I've prayed over and over to God that He would help me eliminate this part of my life, and after many failed attempts at stopping, I just wind up frustrated, with all hope lost of ever completely being freed. This secret has kept me bound up in chains. I can't go a day without thinking about it, and there's a huge longing in my heart for it to just disappear, so I could live my life without having to worry about it or think about it anymore.

Sometimes I can't enjoy any part of my day all because the thoughts of it keep running through my mind. I've asked God to change my heart so I wouldn't dwell on this anymore, but it's still a huge part of my life, and takes up much of my thoughts. And I guess I'm telling you this because I don't know what else to do. I desperately want it to stop, but trying myself has gotten me nowhere, and I'm losing hope. And I know that you will probably suggest telling someone I'm close to so they can help me. But I feel like I can't do that either. They would be so disappointed in me. God is a big part of my life. I love Him with all my heart, and He's been doing some wonderful things inside of me. Many of my relationships revolve around God, and I guess I'm just afraid that they would feel let down by me and God if they were to know about this ... I feel like if anyone knew, they would criticize me and call me a hypocrite, and they wouldn't understand. I'm already really struggling with how God is viewing this, and how He sees me, and what He thinks of me living like this ... I remember also hearing you read someone's story who became freed of their secret, and how much they've been able to live their life with a wonderful new freedom, and that gave me a glimmer of hope for my secret, but now I'm not so sure ... And so I'm wondering if you had any advice as to how I can get rid of this, what else I could do?

She was hoping for another way. I responded to her with the same direction I give everyone else: I told her that she needed to tell someone. There was no getting around it. I told her she could start the process by emailing me her secret. A few weeks later I got this email:

Thank you for writing me back. And so here is my secret: Hmm where to start? I guess I'll just come out with it ... So I have been kind of insecure about myself. I've been hating the person I am, I mean REALLY hating myself, everything about my personality, who I am, and what I do with my time ... and a big one ... the way I look ...

And I guess that there's something inside of me that thinks that I'm only worth as much as the way my body looks, and I have to look a certain way to get anything out of life. I've let myself think that I have to be skinny in order for me to really live and have real joy. So I've formed the habit of ... throwing up after almost every meal. It's one of those parts of myself that I really hate. And at first it was about the skinny thing, and wanting to have that kind of body ... but then it turned into something else. Then it turned into a way to escape the way I was feeling. I guess when I would feel overwhelmed or depressed, or not good enough, I would just start to eat ... and so I would eat and feel full, and with that feeling full I guess it made me feel satisfied in a way, and then everything I was going through didn't seem as bad. But then I'd feel guilty about eating and so I'd go throw it all up, and I'd feel even better about feeling "empty" or "hungry" because it was getting rid of my sin kind of. And so after all that, I wouldn't feel bad about myself anymore. But then it started taking over my whole life, and I would make it a habit, and with everything I did, I would think, ok what am I going to eat and will I be able to go throw it up?

I've even thought that maybe it would be better to be dead than have to live with all my junk, just because most of the time I'm depressed about it, and think that even with God, there's no relief, and it's weird because on the outside, I put off this joyful vibe and people tell me that I'm such a joyful person, but on the inside I'm dying.

As hard as it is to say, I guess I am an addict. And so I do need to tell someone. And yes it scares me to death, but if I want to get better, it's what has to happen. And so I was wondering if you could pray for me since now you're the only one who knows? Just that God would really be here for me to comfort and assure me, to free me from my horrible thoughts about death and not really wanting to live all that much, and that I would be free from throwing up constantly … that I would know what to do next, and who to tell, and that I wouldn't hide this anymore?

—Hillary

I knew we were making progress. Hillary was beginning to experience the value of light in the once dark corner of her heart. For her next baby step I connected her with Noelle, a girl who had also dealt with an eating disorder. After meeting with her for a while, Hillary sent me this email:

After a couple of months, I knew that I needed to tell a couple of my really good friends but I didn't want to. I was so afraid that if I told them, they would leave me and not want to be my friends anymore. I thought the shame I felt about my secret meant that they would be ashamed of me too. One day the Lord gave me the courage and I told my best friend I had to tell her something that was really difficult for me. After I told her my secret, she gave me a huge hug and told me that she honestly didn't see me any differently and that she still loved me. Now I can tell her when I am having a hard day or she'll ask me how I am doing and we pray together about it. To be loved and accepted in something I felt so ashamed about was huge. Now I am not in it alone.

Hillary is doing well today. She's had a few setbacks, but instead of despair there is hope. Instead of death there is life. This email says it all:

After meetings with Noelle I realized that what was going on wasn't really about food at all. It was something bigger than that, something a lot bigger … I was living a lie in a world that is overcome with sinful desires and never is satisfied. Not long ago, I was walking and talking to God as I watched the sunset and I heard His gentle voice say that I was enough for Him, exactly the way I am, I have always been enough for Him. He held me, and in that moment I looked upon the eyes of my true Father, and began to realize that in His eyes, I'm perfect, He doesn't see all the "faults" I see in myself and worry about and work to change, He sees His beautiful daughter who He made for His wonderful plan, and delights in who He made me to be, and just how much He loves it when I am ME. The Spirit changed the way I think, He changed my thoughts, He enabled me to see myself not through the eyes of the world, but through His eyes, the eyes of TRUTH.

(**"I FEEL MOST ALONE WHEN I AM WITH MY FRIENDS."**)

What is it that you have never told a soul? Maybe writing it down is the first step for you. Put your secret on paper, expose it to the air, and get it out of the confines of your heart.

This tiny spark of courage will smolder and grow into reality when you tell your secret to another. Imagine what it would be like to have no secrets. Imagine a world without the weight, the worry, or the fear of exposure.

No more secrets ... freedom is coming.

REFLECTION

/// Have you confessed your secret(s) to another person?

Why or why not?

/// Have you denied, deflected, minimized, or rationalized in a confession?

If so, in what ways?

/// Do you have a heart posture of humility that makes it easy to confess, or are you quick to think you can make it on your own?

4

CONFESS TO THE RIGHT PEOPLE

In high school I had a Swatch watch. The Swatch watch was a plastic watch and band, each with unique neon and pastel designs. Some had crooked second hands, others were geometric, and some were pink, but all Swatch watches were ultra cool.

My watch had a clear casing that showed all the inner workings and gears. Swatch watches also featured the important "Swatch Guard," which was a rubber-band-like contraption that fit over the face to protect against scratches. The watches cost $35–50 and were must-haves for insecure high schoolers.

While I was in high school, my parents finished the basement of our home and installed a phone line in my future bedroom. I was really moving up in the world. I was going to have the whole basement to myself. With the new room and phone line came the important task of buying a phone. So I went to the mall and started my search for the perfect phone.

As I meandered through the phone sections at Sears and Kmart, I found only generic-looking adult phones—the oblong one that came in a multitude of colors or phones with gigantic numbers made for people with poor eyesight. Hoping to find something that fit my personality, I eventually made my way to another store. As I perused the different options, everything started to look the same, until I saw the Swatch logo. *What was a watch doing in the phone section?* I thought. Unbeknownst to me, Swatch also made phones. Different shapes, colors, and sizes ... *but all cool.* Immediately I knew: I was going to be the coolest kid in class. Not only did I have a clear Swatch with a teal Swatch Guard, but now I would have an official Swatch phone as well. This was turning into an incredible day.

Narrowing my options, I gravitated toward a black phone with an angled handpiece. Just as I was about to pick up the box and take it to the counter, I noticed something. The phone right next to it looked identical, but it had an added feature: One could speak into both the base and the receiver. It was amazing! I pictured having a friend over to spend the night and calling another friend on the phone. We could both be on the same phone at the same time.

However, when I picked up the double phone's box and looked at the price tag, I saw that it was twenty dollars more than the one without the upgrade. This wasn't in the budget, but I had to have this phone. So I peeled the price tag off the less expensive phone, put it on the more expensive one, and confidently walked to the counter.

The cashier asked, "Is this going to be all for you?"

"Yep," I responded nonchalantly.

A few pushed buttons, a couple of dings on the cash register, then I slid some cash across the counter, and the box went in a bag with a "Here you are. Have a nice day."

Wow. My ruse had worked. And with that I headed home with my newfound treasure. It looked beautiful next to my bed. It was just waiting to be noticed and admired.

A few weeks later my mom came into my room and asked me, "Aaron, how much did you pay for that phone?"

Oh, no. What is going on here?

"Sixty dollars," I lied.

"Is that how much it cost?" my mom inquired.

To this day I have no idea how she knew what I'd done, but it reinforced my belief that all mothers have superhuman powers, one of which is the ability to know everything that their sons do without a word ever being uttered to them.

"No, it cost eighty dollars." I gulped. My übercoolness was fading quickly with every second that passed. The dream was over.

My mom told me how disappointed she was while I waited for her to hand down my punishment. I knew that it would be big.

Then she said, "I want you to go back to the store and tell them what you did and pay the difference."

Whoa. This was worse than anything I could have imagined. *What were they going to do? Call the police? Charge me 1,000 percent interest? Send me to jail?* I was horrified. I would do anything else, just not that. The embarrassment was going to be too much to handle.

After packaging the phone back up in the box and retrieving the receipt, I drove to the mall and started the long walk to the counter. I started to think that this might not be too bad. *Actually this could be a good thing. I could be labeled a hero. In a culture where integrity is on the decline, perhaps this could be a shining moment. Maybe I would be thanked for being such a young man of character.*

I placed the box and the receipt on the counter and explained my actions. I concluded with "So I am here to make my wrong right." I was waiting for the cheers and the applause.

"I am going to have to go get a manager" was the response.

After what felt like a millennium, a manager made her way out from the back. She asked me to explain myself, and she wasn't smiling. She punched some numbers into the register and coldly said, "That will be twenty dollars and sixty-three cents."

I placed the money on the counter after which she said, "Thank you, and don't ever do that again."

This experience, painful and embarrassing as it was, ended up being an incredible gift to me. It taught me an invaluable lesson: *When possible and appropriate, confession must be done to the one who has been wronged.*

"I AM OVERCOME WITH JEALOUSY."

RESTITUTION

The Bible talks more about confessing to others than it does about confessing to God. We must not forget the need to confess to God as a step toward repentance, but we must also tell someone else. Much of our Christian culture advises us to tell God and be forgiven, or maybe even just tell a spiritual leader (such as a pastor or priest); but the Bible teaches us to go to a much more demanding and uncomfortable place.

Consider the following passage from Numbers 5:

> The LORD said to Moses, "Say to the Israelites: 'When a man or woman wrongs another in any way and so is unfaithful to the LORD, that person is guilty and must confess the sin he has committed. He must make full restitution for his wrong, add one fifth to it and give it all to the person he has wronged.'" (vv. 5–7)

God knows that His people will disobey the law and hurt one another, so He tells us to confess to Him, confess to the one who was wronged, and also to give back what was taken … *and more.*

In Matthew 5:23–24, Jesus says, "Therefore, if you are offering your gift at the altar and there remember that your brother has something against you, leave your gift there in front of the altar. First go and be reconciled to your brother; then come and offer your gift."

Here Jesus shows us that confessing your sin to the one you wronged is both an Old *and* New Testament directive.

Later, in Luke 19, we see that Jesus is not interested only in confession to God or even to a spiritual leader. Zacchaeus was a short, wealthy tax collector who had worked his way to the top by swindling money from the people of Jerusalem. Zacchaeus had an encounter with Jesus that changed his life and resulted in recognition of his sin. Zacchaeus said, "Look, Lord! Here and now I give half of my possessions to the poor, and if I have cheated anybody out of anything, I will pay back four times the amount" (v. 8).

Notice how Jesus doesn't say to him, "Oh, Zacchaeus, don't worry about that, just tell Me and one of My disciples."

Instead, Jesus says that salvation had come to Zacchaeus (v. 9).

(**"I WAS RAPED AND NOW I HAVE SEX WITH NO CARES."**)

IT CAN'T BE ALL ABOUT YOU

Confession to the person you've wronged brings about restitution. The Webster's definition of restitution is "a giving back to the rightful owner of something that has been lost or taken away; restoration." In this way, confession becomes about both the confessor and the one who was wronged. Confession isn't just about having a clear conscience. Confession is about making things right; it's about *restoration*. And God is all about restoration.

I have had lively debates with friends over questions like "Should a cheating spouse tell their spouse what they have done if they have the help they need? Won't it preserve the family if the spouse doesn't know?" The reality is that the truth must be told, not just to a pastor or accountability partner but also to the spouse whose trust was betrayed. Without honesty, the trust in any relationship isn't real!

Confessing our sins allows us to build authentic trust that leads to true intimacy.

Some might reply: "But I will create a huge mess by letting the wronged parties know about my sin. Aaron, your Swatch story is child's play compared to the mess I would make and the people I would hurt."

The key is to understand that, as Andy Stanley said, "confession doesn't hurt people, sin and concealment hurt people."

WHO ARE THE WRONG PEOPLE?

Confession to the person you sinned against is not always the best option though. There's nothing right about a guy confessing to a girl about his lustful thoughts of her. On the other hand, it is right for a husband to confess to his spouse that he looked at pornography. It might not be smart for an employee to confess her hatred for her boss to his face; though a student should confess cheating to a teacher.

So how do we determine who are the right people and who are the wrong people? What if it isn't a secret sin against someone else but a deep-seated fear or something that was done to us? Here are some important filters to determine what will be most productive.

First, if the secret involves someone to whom you have submitted yourself under authority, then the confession should be made to that person. For example, spouses should expose the secrets of their hearts to one another, and children should expose their hearts to their parents. If the secret or sin involves some situation at school, the student could confess to his teacher. If it involves work, an employee could confess to his employer. If it involves church, then a church member could confess to his pastor, as it's appropriate.

It is also vital that you confess to someone trustworthy.

Proverbs 11:13 says, "He who goes about as a talebearer reveals secrets, but he who is trustworthy conceals a matter" (NASB). And in Proverbs 20:19, it says, "A gossip betrays a confidence; so avoid a man who talks too much." Trustworthy people will not gossip about you but rather seek to help you. Perhaps they will even know the proper circumstances and people who can help you. And they won't share your secret to slander you but only out of a desire to help you.

It is unwise to confess to someone of the opposite sex (unless it's your spouse), especially about secrets or sins of a sexual nature. *Why?* Sharing a deep secret is much different than exchanging pleasantries about the weather or the ball game. To expose your heart to someone is to share the depths of your soul and to cultivate trust. Sharing on this level of depth can develop an intimacy that may not be desirable.

Proverbs 13:20 says, "He who walks with the wise grows wise, but a companion of fools suffers harm." Too often I hear about groups of guys who hold each other accountable regarding lust issues: viewing pornography, masturbation, or unhealthy relationships with girls. The problem here is that all of them are dealing with the same problems. So what happens when someone in the group confesses? Nothing! It's difficult for the others to offer helpful advice for reaching future freedom when they're stuck in the quagmire too. I do think it's important to confess your faults to a peer group, regardless of their success in the matter; but in the end it's important to find someone who can actually help and offer experiential advice. Confessing only to someone who can't help just eases your conscience. As the wisdom of Proverbs suggests, be with those who are wise or have figured some things out so you can grow in wisdom and help others as well.

Matthew 7:6 says, "Do not give dogs what is sacred; do not throw your pearls to pigs. If you do, they may trample them under their feet, and then turn and tear you to pieces."

In high school I confessed a secret to a friend who told someone else and then brought it up as a joke at a party. I tried to act like it was no big deal, but I was humiliated. The person to whom you tell your secrets should be mature enough to know not to hurt you with your confession.

(**"I HAVE BEGUN TO HAVE AN EATING DISORDER. MY GREATEST FEAR IN LIFE IS GETTING FAT."**)

Big Difference

Do you know people who tell you secrets like they're informing you of the mileage on their cars? A guy once told me about his secret life of homosexuality in a way that felt like someone placing a data report on a table. Is this what confession to others is all about? Simply getting the information out?

When God calls us to confession, it's not just about sharing details for the purpose of information transference. To better understand what God has called us to, it is important to know the difference between *transparency* and *vulnerability.*

Transparency is sharing the intimate details of your life with another. Vulnerability is going beyond transparency to invite others *into* the details of your life and asking them to help you.

The reason there are right and wrong people to whom we should confess our secrets and sins has to do with so much more than information. Rather it has to do with an invitation and where the confession goes with that person once it's been confessed.

Transparency is a start, but vulnerability is what God is interested in for us. Transparency is about you, while vulnerability is about you *and others.* Confession to others is about inviting the help and strength of others into your situation. This is more than just semantics; it's about the difference between humility and pride, between isolation and community, and between your strength and God's strength. And these differences make all the difference in the world.

(**"I THINK MY LIFE IS BORING SO I MAKE UP STORIES TO MAKE MY LIFE SOUND COOL."**)

TEMPTATIONS

The power of confession isn't about restitution alone—it can also serve as a powerful tool to keep us from developing secrets. Confession connects us to the grace of God, which empowers us to live holy and righteous lives. Jude 24 starts out, "To him [God] who is able to keep you from falling … "

He is the God who not only restores and reconciles but also keeps us from messes in the first place. What would happen if we simply confessed our temptations? Maybe we would have fewer sins to confess.

I used to have a problem with lying. After the price-tag-switching incident, while in college, I forged a professor's signature to get into a closed class, and I once gave a false name on a sign-in sheet to avoid a grade reduction due to excessive tardiness (I got caught and paid a much higher price).

Then the Holy Spirit convicted me of my sins.

I decided to stay as far away from deception as possible and confess even the temptation to hide truth in any way. A simple statement like "I was thinking about cheating on my financial-management exam" brought my deception into the open and removed the power from the temptation (cheating wouldn't have helped me in that class anyway!). Because I haven't struggled with this in a long time, the temptation now seems laughable. However, every time I am tempted to lie now, I still share it with my wife. Confessing my temptations in this way keeps me further from sin, and I find myself confessing fewer instances of deceit.

("I HAVE CHEATED ON MY GIRLFRIEND THREE TIMES. I HAVEN'T TOLD GOD OR ASKED FOR FORGIVENESS.")

One time I was staying in a hotel during a ministry trip. After watching TV one evening in my room, I called my wife and told her about a love scene in a show I had watched. I confessed not because I'd done anything wrong, given in to any temptation or lust, or violated her in any way, rather I wanted to make sure any temptation was brought into the light. Because light kills darkness.

I have a friend who was a sex addict. Even after being free for years, he immediately called a friend when he saw the *P* on the cover of a *Playboy* magazine in the carry-on bag of a guy sitting next to him on an airplane. All he saw was the *P*, and he called to confess the temptation that came his way. Sound extreme? Certainly, but he doesn't want anything to take root in his heart.

Temptations themselves can be secrets that grow (see James 1:15: "After desire has conceived, it gives birth to sin"), but confessing your temptations can prevent them from sprouting, gaining traction, and leading you to a place you never wanted to go.

I've talked with people who have learned about the power of confession and found it easy to share their past secrets, but have difficulty confessing their present secrets. Confession isn't just about the past. Rather confession is about the secret that might be an all-out war today. To tell someone about the struggle you're having requires the humility to say, "I haven't gotten this under control and need help." To confess is to say, "I am weak." It is in this weakness that God is strong.

REFLECTION

/// Do you need to confess to a person you have wronged?

/// Have you confessed to the right people?

/// Are you vulnerable with others or merely transparent?

/// What temptations should you confess?

5

THE LOST ART OF CONFESSION

When I think of confession, the image that comes to mind is of a wooden booth inside a stone cathedral with magnificent artwork, hard pews, and a lot of stained glass. A black curtain serves as the door, and the booth is divided by a wall with a small screen that allows for communication between the two sides. A priest sits on one side, patiently listening to whoever needs to unload in anonymity.

Sound familiar?

On a trip around Europe several years ago with my wife, we found ourselves in a lifetime's worth of cathedrals. I was excited when I saw one that had a booth I could go into. There wasn't a priest on the other side that day, but I did feel like I was transported into a movie (which is the only other place I've seen a confessional booth in action—often as a place where a criminal on the run finds himself). The dialogue in the movie might have gone something like this: "Bless me, Father, for I have sinned. It has been however many weeks [or years] since my last confession." After a particularly hesitant and brief confession the priest responds with a compassionate and absolving tone, "Your sins are forgiven."

This practice may have lost traction in many Catholic churches and been rejected entirely by most Protestant churches, but though the wooden booth and the metal screen may be gone, should the practice really be lost?

As you read the previous chapters, did you feel like rejecting the idea of confession? Maybe you think that it's a practice for Catholics only, which ignores the fact that with Jesus as our mediator we have direct access to God and we don't need a priest or anyone else for confession. Though it's true that we don't need a person to act as a bridge between us and God, I wonder if we have thrown the baby out with the bathwater.

Let's take a look at the evolution of confession in church history and see what emerges.

(**"I CAN'T FORGIVE THEM (EVEN THOUGH I TELL EVERYONE THAT I ALREADY DID)."**)

HISTORY

Perhaps the booth I described earlier is also the first thing that pops into your mind when you hear the word *confession*. But the truth is, the confessional booth is a relatively new fixture in church history.

Saint Charles Borromeo introduced the confessional in 1577. He was the archbishop of Milan and a prominent figure in the Counter-Reformation. He published a set of architectural rules for churches that included the three-sided structure to be constructed in an open area of the church, with some to include kneelers. The confessor (or penitent) was supposed to face in the direction of the altar. The design became very popular, and by the end of the sixteenth century confessionals could be found in nearly every Catholic church.[12]

Though the confessional booth as we know it is relatively new, the practice of confession is not. The process and the theology have simply evolved.

After the writings of the apostles in the Bible, the sacrament of confession was mentioned by Tertullian, a second-century church father:

> Prostrate yourself at the feet of the priests and kneel before the beloved of God, making all the brethren commissioned ambassadors of your prayer for pardon.[13]

The act of prostration, or kneeling before a priest, is still held and practiced in the Orthodox Church. The confessor sits or stands next to the priest in front of an icon of Christ, signifying that it is Christ who hears and forgives the transgression and the priest is merely a witness.

Not long after Tertullian wrote about confession, priests began assigning penitents to periods of exclusion from the Eucharist (Communion), depending on the sins they had committed. For more serious or grave sins, seven years of exclusion from Communion was not uncommon.

The Canons of Hippolytus, written in Rome around AD 230, state the following about the sin of murder: "If anyone has shed [human] blood, let him not take part in the [eucharistic] mysteries, unless he has been purified by a punishment, by tears and groans."

(**"I FEAR MYSELF MORE THAN ANYONE ELSE."**)

Although public confession was encouraged and could affect your ability to participate in the Eucharist, it wasn't regulated by any formal code until the fourth century. In AD 313 at the Council of Elvira held in Spain, we see the earliest example of the discipline of confession moving toward the penance and absolution of sins.

In the sixth century, Pope Gregory the Great grew concerned with how to offer God satisfaction for sins that were committed. He believed:

> This is done through penance, which consists of contrition, confession, and the actual punishment or satisfaction. To these must be added priestly absolution, which confirms the forgiveness granted by God. Those who die in the faith and communion of the church, but without having offered satisfaction for all their sins, will go to purgatory before they attain their final salvation.[14]

Then in the thirteenth century, Pope Innocent III reformed the church through the decrees of the Fourth Lateran Council, which focused on intense micromanagement and control of the personal confessions and inner lives of believers. The council decided that the faithful must confess their sins at least once a year.

This kind of regulation and increased abuse of confession as a tool of manipulation by the Roman Catholic Church continued in the fourteenth, fifteenth, and sixteenth centuries. It came to a head with the selling of indulgences. An indulgence was a payment to the Catholic Church that purchased an exemption from punishment (penance) for certain types of sins. Indulgences became like "confession insurance" against eternal damnation. If you purchased an indulgence, then you wouldn't go to hell if you died suddenly or forgot to confess a sin. This connection between confession and penance to salvation ultimately fueled the fires of the Reformation.

The Reformation moved Protestant believers back to a form of private confession that stayed between God and the believer. The following proclamation was made at the Ecumenical Council of Trent (1545–1563), which condemned the Protestant movement as heretical:

> As the frailty and weakness of human nature are universally known and felt … no one can be ignorant of the paramount necessity of the Sacrament of Penance. Its exposition demands an accuracy superior to that of Baptism. Baptism is administered but once, and can not be repeated; Penance may be administered, and becomes necessary, as often as we may have sinned after Baptism…. For those

who fall into sin after Baptism … the Sacrament of
Penance is as necessary to salvation as is Baptism for
those who have not already been baptized.[15]

In 1907, the Catholic Church again confirmed this position, in a
decree by Pope Pius X called *"Lamentabili sane,"* by condemning the
following propositions, calling them "errors of the modernists":

In the primitive [early] Church the concept of
the Christian sinner reconciled by the authority
of the Church did not exist. Only very slowly did
the Church accustom herself to this concept. As a
matter of fact, even after Penance was recognized
as an institution of the Church, it was not called
a Sacrament since it would be held as a disgraceful
Sacrament.

The words of the Lord, "Receive the Holy
Spirit; whose sins you shall forgive, they are forgiven them; and whose sins you shall retain, they
are retained" (John 20:22–23), in no way refer
to the Sacrament of Penance, in spite of what it
pleased the Fathers of Trent to say.[16]

(**"SOMETIMES I WISH SUICIDE WAS OKAY
(WRITING THIS MAKES ME WANT TO LIVE)."**)

LITURGY

Oscar Wilde once said, "It is the confession, not the priest, that gives us absolution." In resisting the need for a priest, the role of confession in the lives of many believers diminished. Catholic churches are actively training followers in the value of confession, but as personal independence continues to increase, the lines to confessionals will steadily decrease.

(**"MY DAD LEFT AND I DON'T MISS HIM."**)

Throughout the centuries, Christian liturgy has dictated that Communion follows confession. Usually there is a time of silence dedicated to personal confession and then a corporate confession, which may sound something like this:

"Most merciful God, we confess that we have sinned against you in thought, word, and deed, by what we have done, and by what we have left undone. We have not loved you with our whole heart; we have not loved our neighbors as ourselves. We are truly sorry and we humbly repent. For the sake of your Son Jesus Christ, have mercy on us and forgive us; that we may delight in your will, and walk in your ways, to the glory of your Name. Amen."[17]

I also like this corporate confessional prayer, as it includes modern sins and temptations:

"Father, we confess that we are sinners and that we have sinned.... We are guilty of having itching ears. We have failed to receive and proclaim the truth; we have wandered off into myths; we have listened to and preached a false gospel of self-improvement, self-reliance, and self-righteousness because it suited our passions. We cry to You now for mercy and forgiveness. Fill our hearts and minds with a passion for the gospel of redemption through Christ alone. Teach us to be faithful witnesses of Your grace and to serve each other humbly, compassionately, and faithfully. In the name of our crucified and risen Savior, amen."

Depending on your church tradition, you may never have participated in a corporate liturgical reading like this. The order of the service isn't what matters though. The purpose of confession goes far beyond the individual. It isn't meant to make the penitent "feel good" or to clear his or her conscience. Instead confession is a reminder of our constant need for grace.

> One Sunday afternoon in the 1930's in a little parish in Germany where he was pastor, Father Häring was leading the customary Sunday afternoon parish Vesper service with religious instruction and Benediction. This particular Sunday he was talking about confession.
>
> "What is the most important thing about confession?" he asked. A woman in the front pew responded: "Telling your sins to the priest. That's why we call it *confession*." Father Häring said, "Confessing the sins is important, but it's not the *most* important thing." A man towards the back called out: "Contrition! Being sorry for your sins!

The whole thing doesn't work without contrition." Father Häring said, "True, it doesn't 'work' without contrition; but I don't think contrition is *the most important* thing." A man over on St. Joseph's side spoke up: "It's the examination of conscience. Unless you examine your conscience, you don't know what you have to be sorry for and what to confess." Father Häring still wasn't satisfied.

An uneasy silence fell over the church. Then a little girl in the second pew said: "Father, I know what is most important. It's what Jesus does!"

It's what Jesus does! That's the most important thing, the thing we should focus upon. The examination of conscience, sorrow for sin, telling the sins to the priest—these are all important. But you will have a more positive experience of the sacrament if your focus is on *what Jesus does.*[18]

(**"I HAVE BEEN TEMPTED BY HOMOSEXUALITY SINCE I WAS 5 AND I AM STILL STRUGGLING AT AGE 23."**)

Something incredible happens when we admit sin and embrace weakness. Paul said, "In my weakness Christ is made strong" (see 2 Cor. 12:5–10). The act of confession makes clear not only our own inadequacy, but it also proclaims God's supremacy. In a culture that promotes avoiding weakness at all costs, it is good to be reminded of our desperate need for God. We don't need reminders of our greatness as much as we need reminders of our weakness. Maybe we should spend less time focusing on our self-esteem and more time reinforcing God's work in us. Instead of buying into a perspective that says we need to be strong at all costs, let's go the opposite way and fall on the altar of God's mercy, sufficiency, and forgiveness through Jesus.

Without a belief in the necessity of confession, we have cheapened the gospel and the power of the cross. Dietrich Bonhoeffer once said:

> Cheap grace is the preaching of forgiveness without requiring repentance, baptism without church discipline, Communion without confession, absolution without personal confession.[19]

The greater purpose of confession is to realize the need for God and better understand our size in relation to God. God is big, and we are small. When we forget who is big and who is small, we tend to believe that we are big and therefore must take care of all our problems ourselves.

("I CAN'T FORGIVE MY MOTHER FOR WHAT SHE HAS DONE TO ME. I KNOW I NEED TO FORGIVE HER BUT IT'S TOO HARD.")

COMMUNITY

Without confession, we cannot commune with God or with others. When we hide something, we interrupt those relationships. God made us for communion, so when we do not confess, we miss out on true relationship and community. However, confessing our ultimate need for God and our inability to save ourselves actually unites us with God. Salvation begins with confession, and continued relationship with God requires regular confession as well.

(**"I AM NOT HAPPY."**)

In his book *Celebration of Discipline,* Richard Foster wrote that in recent church history there has been an emphasis on the role of community in confession:

> Confession is a difficult Discipline for us because we all too often view the believing community as a fellowship of saints before we see it as a fellowship of sinners. We feel that everyone else has advanced so far into holiness that we are isolated and alone in our sin. We cannot bear to reveal our failures and shortcomings to others. We imagine that we are the only ones who have not stepped onto the high road to heaven. Therefore, we hide ourselves from one another and live in veiled lies and hypocrisy....

In acts of mutual confession we release the power
that heals. Our humanity is no longer denied, but
transformed.[20]

(**"I HAVE FALLEN SO SHORT. I AM TWO-FACED.
I FEEL LIKE A HYPOCRITE."**)

TODAY

The history of the practice of confession serves to teach us today. Just
as apostles, early church fathers, popes, reformers, and believers in
every age of church history have wrestled with the theological and
practical aspects of confession, we too should seek the heart of this
practice. Though there have been periods when it has taken center
stage and others when it has drifted to the periphery, there is a reason
it's never been completely lost.

Deep within the heart and soul of every person is a God-designed
hunger to live in the light free of sin. We all have a sense that true
freedom is possible and a hope that we can experience it. Frederick
Buechner wrote, "What we hunger for perhaps more than anything
else is to be known in our full humanness, and yet that is often just
what we also fear more than anything else."[21]

Confession is what allows us to be fully known.

REFLECTION

/// Have you dismissed confession because of preconceived notions?

/// What can you learn from the history of confession?

PART 2

WALK IN THE LIGHT

6

NOT SELF-HELP

It might be easy to stop here, put this book down, and think, *Okay I've got it. I confess the secrets of my heart to God with humility and honesty, and then confess to someone mature without excuses or sugarcoating, and finally, I confess to the person I wronged if the situation is right. I'm working up the courage right now and after I do that I will be totally fine. No more problems. All set.*

I wish I could tell you it was that easy, but dealing with our secrets is not about finding the five simple steps to freedom. Confession on its own is not the end at all—it is only the beginning of a journey toward healing, wholeness, and life. Sometimes this journey may seem arduous or mundane, other times simple or full of adventure. But this process is so much more than a list of steps; it is about the posture of our hearts. I pray you are not scared off by what might lie ahead, because the journey from here forward is rich and fulfilling beyond your wildest imagination.

Awhile back at theMILL I taught a series called "Death and All His Friends" about the seven deadly sins: pride, envy, gluttony, greed, sloth, lust, and wrath. There is uncertainty about their origin, but the first known written copy of the seven deadly sins was from a Desert Father named Evagrius Ponticus not long before AD 400. The Desert Fathers were hermits, ascetics, and monks who lived in the deserts of Egypt and abandoned cities of the pagan world to live in solitude. Ponticus's primary purpose was diagnostic in nature; he wanted to identify and classify all of the sin issues that arise in people's lives. His list can also help unearth the seeds of these sins before they start to germinate and grow.

As I personally studied each sin in this list, I thought about how to eliminate, curb, or avoid them. The default easy next step was to provide a list of tips and techniques that can help us "kick the habit," a litany of self-help ideas to deal with personal problems. The danger is that sin then gets classified in psychological terms, which would only require psychological answers; or in physiological terms, which in turn would need physiological solutions; or in social terms, which would demand social answers.

(**"I AM STILL BELIEVING THE LIE THE GIRLS IN JUNIOR HIGH TOLD ME; THAT I'M NOT WORTH ANYTHING."**)

Sometimes tips and techniques seem great because they allow us to take action and feel better. But in reality they don't change much because they don't actually address the roots of the problems. Why? Because the seven deadly sins are not just problems, struggles, or simple mistakes. They are sins! Since sin is not a psychological or physiological problem but a spiritual problem at its core, it requires a spiritual solution.

The self-help market is alive and well—it was an $11 billion industry in 2008. A quick Google search of the term *self-help* will produce a massive list of resources to make your life better, build your self-esteem, manage your anger, find friendships, eliminate stress, develop your intellect, etc. My favorites are books that guarantee happiness with lines like:

> "This is a manual for making your life happier!"
> "Discover the 10 Keys for Maximum Happiness!"
> "You control your happiness. It really is your choice."

Are these for real? Is there actually a manual for happiness? Or would it just contain some pointers on how to avoid negative things and put a smile on your face every once in a while? Couldn't there be a core issue that is causing you not to experience happiness, such as self-hatred, insecurity, judgment, or unforgiveness?

(**"I CANNOT DEVELOP AND MAINTAIN WHOLE-HEARTED HEALTHY RELATIONSHIPS."**)

Tips and techniques are not inherently wrong. It is a good thing to put an Internet filter on your computer to block pornographic websites in the battle against lust, it is wise to avoid alcohol if drunkenness is an issue; however, if we treat tips and techniques as the solutions to our sins, then we put pressure on them to do what they cannot. Why would we think that self-help solutions are going to solve the problems we created in the first place? Maybe we believe that because we created these problems we must fix them ourselves. This idea that help comes to those who help themselves is prevalent in our culture and is reinforced by our celebration of "self-made" millionaires, musicians, and entrepreneurs.

Perhaps because we are impatient and addicted to quick fixes, one-answer solutions, and shortcuts, we love the three steps to a healthy marriage, the four keys to finding your calling, or the top ten ways to financial freedom. These tips may be helpful, but we shouldn't be disappointed when they don't cultivate intimacy in our marriages, develop a true sense of purpose in our lives, or root out the greed that drives us to hoard our wealth. In our attempt to solve our problems, have we traded the best solution for a cheap substitute? Have we exchanged true Holy Spirit empowerment for self-disciplined yet largely ineffective regimens? Have we traded repentance for a complex psychological assessment, intimacy for programmatic structures, or salvation for religion?

We even use this perspective in our approach to the Bible. One of the statements I hear that grates on me is, "I used [insert Scripture verse here] to get [insert desire, need, or dream here]."

Are there promises and helpful guidelines for living biblically? *Yes.* Is the Bible a book of promises and guarantees from God? *No.* To approach Scripture this way is to treat the Bible as a self-help manual with a few cool stories wrapped around some sweet if/then principles. Our culture loves to turn everything into a product. But the Bible isn't a product to be "used" or a book of principles to help us have "better" lives. Rather the Bible is an invitation into *God's* cosmic story of redemption and rescue.

Tips and techniques can't transform a heart or kill sin. Am I saying that we should ditch the helpful tips altogether? No. Instead we should give them the proper roles in our lives. We love to break our problems into small pieces, thinking that if we do so we can easily understand and master them. The key to the Christian life, however, is letting go of control and yielding to the One who can ultimately form true righteousness inside us. Methods and ten-step plans may add to what God has done, but they're no substitute for His work.

A. W. Tozer described our efforts to do God's work like this:

> Powerless religion may put a man through many surface changes and leave him exactly what he was before. The changes are in form only, they are not in kind. Behind the activities of the non-religious man and the man who has received the gospel without power lie the same motives. An unblessed ego lies at the bottom of both lives, the difference being the religious man has learned better to disguise his vice. His sins are refined and less offensive than before he took up religion, but the man himself is not a better man in the sight of God. He may indeed be a worse one, for always God hates artificiality and pretense. Selfishness still throbs like an engine at the center of the man's life. True, he may learn to "redirect" his selfish impulses, but his woe is that self still lives unrebuked and even unsuspected within his deep heart. He is a victim

of religion without power. The man who has received the Word without power has trimmed his hedge, but it is a thorn hedge still and can never bring forth the fruits of the new life.[22]

We can confess the secrets of our hearts, experience a release, and feel lighter, yet still find that we're only going through the motions. Embracing the confess-your-secrets-self-help plan alone isn't a solution. The key is the posture of our hearts. Ultimately we must run from self-help and engage the help of God.

INVISIBLE

I love the definition of *grace* as "God at work."[23] If the opposite is "me at work," then all of life in God is about His active grace in my heart. My life in God is all about letting God do something profound in me—all about God transforming my motives, thoughts, and behavior.

Any step we take on our own should be about creating space for God to do the work that we are incapable of doing. "Once we get this through our heads and assimilated into our imaginations, we are out of the driver's seat forever," wrote Eugene Peterson. "The practice of resurrection [i.e., our personal growth] is not a do-it-yourself self-help project. It is God's project, and he is engaged full-time in carrying it out."[24]

So does that mean that we take a backseat, eat Twinkies, drink Dr Pepper, play video games, and tell God to go for it? *Of course not.* We're not spectators. We are active participants in the work of God. But we aren't in charge. We aren't determining the destination or creating the strategy for our lives. God is.

First Thessalonians 5:23 says, "May God himself, the God of peace, sanctify you through and through." And Colossians 1:16–17 states, "For everything, absolutely everything, above and below, visible and invisible, rank after rank after rank of angels—everything got started in him and finds its purpose in him. He was there before any of it came into existence and holds it all together right up to this moment" (MSG). God does the real work in us! He holds us together, and He is before, in, under, above, through, and beyond it all.

The hardest part to embrace about God's working in us is that we can't see Him working. We love things we can see. When we can see something, we can control it, define the results, and set a timeline. Our culture is addicted to both instant gratification and control, while God frequently works slowly over the course of a lifetime.

To say that confession is the beginning of a journey and not a predictable and measurable self-help program is to embrace the invisible, the uncertain. And isn't that what faith is all about—*the invisible?* Or have we thrown out the invisible and thus thrown out grace?

Nothing New

This approach of treating only the visible symptoms and behavior rather than dealing with the deepest issues of our hearts is not just an American problem. The self-help tendency was in full bloom even when Jesus walked the earth, and He addressed the problem of formulaic holiness very directly. They weren't known as self-help gurus then but Pharisees and teachers of the law. The Pharisees were the religious leaders of the day, and they had the routine down pat. They were actually professionals at how-to programs. They had mastered the art of missing the forest for the trees.

In Matthew 23, Jesus spoke harshly against the Pharisees and teachers of the law. Jesus described their core problem in verses 25 and 26 when He said, "Woe to you, teachers of the law and Pharisees, you hypocrites! You clean the outside of the cup and dish, but inside they are full of greed and self-indulgence. Blind Pharisee! First clean the inside of the cup and dish, and then the outside also will be clean."

Dealing with behavioral issues only requires old-fashioned self-discipline. The Pharisees had that. Jesus was saying that it goes much deeper than that. In the Sermon on the Mount Jesus made a similar point, saying, "You have heard that it was said to the people long ago, 'Do not murder, and anyone who murders will be subject to judgment.' But I tell you that anyone who is angry with his brother will be subject to judgment" (Matt. 5:21–22). In other words, the real test is what's going on in your heart. Do you have hate raging, bitterness festering, unforgiveness simmering, or revenge brewing in your heart? If so, you must address that as sin.

A guy recently asked Daniel, one of the pastors on my staff, for help. This guy was regularly sleeping around, and he said to Daniel, "The *only* problem I have is girls. Everything else in my life works. I only have this one issue. Will you meet with me to help me?" The guy's question was a request for some fast-acting tips and techniques. Daniel could have responded with a series of cup-polishing maneuvers but instead went for the heart.

"I disagree that girls are your only problem," Daniel told him. "In fact, I think that's impossible. Here's why: Wrapped up in your promiscuity are layers of pride, selfishness, lust, and idolatry. I think the promiscuity is a by-product of a more rooted defect in your heart, namely the fact that you have yet to surrender your life to Jesus and die to living a life that is about *you*. So, actually, at this point the promiscuity is pretty normal for the life you've chosen to live, a life of self."

Daniel continued his response. "We often want the consequences of our sin to be taken away; we want to feel better about ourselves without really wanting to be broken and exposed before God on *His* terms. So we gloss over our guilt, hoping for a quick fix from an impersonal God. It doesn't (and it *can't!*) work that way.

"You have to be willing to lose your life. *Everything*.

"So, I am willing to meet with you. I'm not expecting you to change everything overnight. It'll be a process. I just want to make sure we're both pointed in the same direction before moving forward."

"I CAN'T COMMIT TO ANYTHING."

THE CROSS

Recently I heard a girl say, "I just don't know why people make such a big deal about the cross."

At first I was appalled, but then my heart broke. She considered herself a Christian but had essentially embraced a cross-less

Christianity. She believed that following Jesus was about buying into a positive worldview with some generally accepted moral and behavioral guidelines.

Doing good things doesn't make you a Christian. You can volunteer regularly at the soup kitchen, go to church every Sunday, and be a "good person" yet not be any more of a Christian than the guy who gets drunk every weekend and calls himself an atheist. Christianity without the cross is mere moralism: living according to a religious moral code all the while never embracing faith in Jesus.

So why is the cross such a big deal?

Take a few minutes and read these passages of Scripture. Allow your heart to reflect and meditate on the cross:

> For the message of the cross is foolishness to those who are perishing, but to us who are being saved it is the power of God. (1 Cor. 1:18)

> Christ redeemed us from that self-defeating, cursed life by absorbing it completely into himself. Do you remember the Scripture that says, "Cursed is everyone who hangs on a tree"? That is what happened when Jesus was nailed to the cross: He became a curse, and at the same time dissolved the curse. And now, because of that, the air is cleared and we can see that Abraham's blessing is present and available for non-Jews, too. We are all able to receive God's life, his Spirit, in and with us by believing—just the way Abraham received it. (Gal. 3:13–14 MSG)

For my part, I am going to boast about nothing but the Cross of our Master, Jesus Christ. Because of that Cross, I have been crucified in relation to the world, set free from the stifling atmosphere of pleasing others and fitting into the little patterns that they dictate. Can't you see the central issue in all this? It is not what you and I do—submit to circumcision, reject circumcision. It is what God is doing, and he is creating something totally new, a free life! All who walk by this standard are the true Israel of God—his chosen people. Peace and mercy on them! (Gal. 6:14–16 MSG)

Entering into this fullness is not something you figure out or achieve. It's not a matter of being circumcised or keeping a long list of laws. No, you're already in—insiders—not through some secretive initiation rite but rather through what Christ has already gone through for you, destroying the power of sin. If it's an initiation ritual you're after, you've already been through it by submitting to baptism. Going under the water was a burial of your old life; coming up out of it was a resurrection, God raising you from the dead as he did Christ. When you were stuck in your old sin-dead life, you were incapable of responding to God. God brought you alive—right along with Christ! Think of it! All sins forgiven, the

slate wiped clean, that old arrest warrant can-
celed and nailed to Christ's cross. He stripped all
the spiritual tyrants in the universe of their sham
authority at the Cross and marched them naked
through the streets. (Col. 2:11–15 MSG)

Incredible!

We are inherently sinful and need to be saved from the destructive effects of our sin. We need to be saved from death. The cross
is God's answer to our need. The cross doesn't take us from bad to
good but from dead to alive! The power and vitality of the cross to
walking in freedom (both temporally and eternally) is at the core of
all that we believe. Without the cross we have nothing.

Is the cross fundamental to your faith? What would happen if
the cross were removed from your walk with God? Would anything
change?

There is no better place to engage God, who is the spiritual solution to our spiritual problems, than at the cross. It is there that Christ
dealt with the spiritual condition of humanity. To eliminate the cross
from our discussion of freedom is to eliminate the football from the
Super Bowl. *It cannot be done.*

REPENTANCE

So how do we engage the cross? The simple answer: *repentance.*

And the door to repentance is confession. Confession is the
statement that says, "I can't do it on my own. I am responsible for
what I have done, and I need help." Confession is the admission of a
need. Repentance is engaging God as the answer.

Repentance isn't just a flippant "Sorry." Repentance entails a deep sorrow. Second Corinthians 7:10–11 describes cross-centered repentance: "Godly sorrow brings repentance that leads to salvation and leaves no regret, but worldly sorrow brings death. See what this godly sorrow has produced in you: what earnestness, what eagerness to clear yourselves, what indignation, what alarm, what longing, what concern, what readiness to see justice done."

Repentance places the cross at the center of our road to freedom, and the cross is what puts God's grace at the beginning, middle, and end of our entire lives.

(
"I USE MY FRIENDSHIPS FOR MY OWN SELF-ISH GAIN."
)

Take a look at this email entitled "a testimony of grace," which I received from a girl during a series of talks I did on repentance:

Hey Pastor Aaron,

Just wanted to share with you a bit of what God has been doing in me over the past couple of months.

My family's motto has been one of hurt and anger; physical, emotional, sexual, and verbal abuse are tools of the trade. Needless to say I have been holding a lot of anger, bitterness, and pure hatred inside of me for a long time.

The past few years have been intense. I have given up and traded God, family, and friends for alcohol, nicotine, sex, work, and anything that might be big enough to fill the void. Anything to hide my pain behind.

I would say that I have been a casualty of religion, never understanding the realness of a relationship with the Messiah. My knowledge of what I thought I knew was just enough to never understand the reality of Jesus.

These last few weeks I have been shattered! Psalm 51 has been my reality. Broken I have come before my Savior finally understanding a minute bit about grace. The understanding of my humanity, the way I have put myself on God's throne saying I am better than He.

I have been so unforgiving toward my dad. I realized I've done such horrid things to God and received unfathomable forgiveness. How could I continue to turn around and be unforgiving? So tonight I spoke the words out loud. Not by my will but with God working in me.

I have only begun this process of progressive sanctification. I have a feeling it is going to be a hard and tedious journey, but I am on the road to recovery. I am being remade. I know there is so much more to my story and God has only begun.

Stephanie

She got it! Confession led to repentance, and God is at work! Since this email I have seen an incredible transformation in Stephanie happen before my eyes. She is growing and becoming healthy from the inside out. She hasn't embraced a formula for "successful Christian living." She tried that already ... this time around she's embracing grace.

THE SLIPPERY SLOPE

Why do we embrace self-help solutions so quickly?

Though self-help Christianity has been around for thousands of years, there are some deep-rooted tendencies that keep it alive. At the core of it all, we are selfish beings and we believe we are at the center of the universe, not God. When we think we can fix everything ourselves, we actually glorify ourselves above God.

I don't think that we make this flying leap in one bounding step. Subtle shifts in perspectives and beliefs cause us to believe that the condition of our hearts isn't a big deal.

First, we don't really believe that we're sinful. We have some weaknesses, sure, but sins—*nope.* Sin is reserved for the Charles Mansons, Ted Bundys, and Adolf Hitlers of the world ... and I'm not one of them. I'm a good person. I make mistakes and have weaknesses, but I'm working on it.

Second, we regularly give ourselves the benefit of the doubt. We judge ourselves based on our intentions, not on our actions. We tell ourselves, "I don't have a sin issue. I just struggle now and then. My sin doesn't deserve wrath ... maybe a scolding or a slap on the wrist, but death?"

At the same time we begin to take some liberties with our view of God. "I know that God hates sin, but He responds to sin with love, not judgment. I prefer to see Him as a God of love and toler-ance. And if He is a God of love then He really isn't that bothered by my 'struggles.' He understands my heart and will give me an A for effort."

(
   "I AM AFRAID OF NEVER FINDING SOMEONE WHO WILL LOVE ME FOR ME."
)

In this way we begin to believe that only "bad people" sin, we dirty up our image of God, while simultaneously cleaning up our image of ourselves. This combination is lethal. Now in our minds God is no longer a holy God who hates sin, and we are no longer sinful people who are helpless apart from God.

This response is completely backward. God is not our self-help guru, available to use when we need Him. God is not someone we're trying to fit into *our* world in order to "bless" our relationships, our careers, our finances, or to help us kick some bad habits. Sin is not reserved for those on death row. We are not good enough on our own. We need to be rescued. We can't fix ourselves, we can't make our own way, and we are not the center of the universe.

We must see sin as it is, God for who He is, and ourselves as we truly are. That's where our hearts and grace collide, and freedom begins.

REFLECTION

/// Do you find yourself focusing on behavioral modification or heart transformation?

/// In what ways can you provide space for God to work in you?

/// Are you living a cross-less Christianity in any way?

/// What is your view of God?

/// How do you view yourself and your sinfulness?

7

MOTIVATION FOR THE JOURNEY

John had secrets. He had secrets about girls—how he treated them and what he thought about them. Secret interactions he had with them both in person and in cyberspace.

At first, John didn't really like the idea, but eventually he decided to go down the road of confession. He told a few trusted friends and me about his lust, his warped perspective of women, and the ways he abused them. He was brutally honest and open with us and put it all out there for us to see.

After a few rounds of this kind of confession, he came to me and said, "I'm still struggling. Where is the freedom in this? I feel like I have walked out of the darkness. It feels great to get things into the open and to know that I'm not living with the weight of hiding my secrets. I'm thankful for the forgiveness of God and know that telling others, no matter how embarrassed I have felt, is a good thing. But I feel like I'm confessing new secrets all the time. Is this really how it's supposed to be?"

As I mentioned earlier, freedom is a journey. Coming out of the dark by using confession to shine the light of God into the shadows of our hearts is just the beginning of the journey. Along the way, we embrace the invisible work of the Holy Spirit and engage the grace of God to do what we cannot. I know plenty of people like John who confessed their secrets, exposed the recesses of their hearts, and within months, weeks, or even days, found themselves repeating the cycle they had hoped to escape. Feeling stuck once again and disappointed that things weren't fixed, they ask, "Why am I still dealing with this? I thought confession was supposed to set me free. I thought this was the end of darkness at work in me. Did I do something wrong?"

Sometimes these questions lead to even bigger questions and thoughts—the kind that can be faith shaking.

"Maybe God isn't really able to help me. Did God forget about me? Am I not worth it?"

(**"I HAVE JEALOUSY AND TRUST ISSUES WITH MEN. I HAVE NEVER TOLD MY HUSBAND."**)

RELIEF

I love living in Colorado. One reason I love it here is because of all the things I can do outside. The Rocky Mountains are an outdoor enthusiast's playground—snowboarding, mountain biking, rock climbing, white-water rafting, etc. Risk, adventure, and enjoying God's magnificent creation! However, taking part in these sports over the years has taken a toll on my body. I have separated my shoulder

flying off a ski jump, slammed into trees going full speed on a mountain bike, and visited the emergency room a few times. The greatest
damage of all this activity has been on my back. My vertebrae have
been rearranged countless times, which has earned me frequent visits
to the chiropractor's office.

On my first visit I was shown a "road to recovery" chart. It was
a picture of the journey ahead of me on the road to spinal recovery.
The journey has an upward trajectory. The beginning is at the place
of pain that brought me to the chiropractor in the first place, and it
is followed by a steady movement away from the pain toward relief
after regular adjustments. Around the halfway point in this journey
there is a moment of decision. It's when I feel good, I'm not bent over
in pain, and I feel dramatically different than my first visit. I can do
just about everything I am used to doing, and I no longer feel pain
when I'm physically active. I asked my doctor about this point, and
he said it is here that the majority of a chiropractor's patients quit ...
but they will return. Why? Quitting halfway results in a slow return
to pain. They didn't complete the journey as outlined on the chart.
The chart shows that for lasting improvement, people must continue
getting adjusted to strengthen their backs, even when the pain is
gone. Building strength and developing healthy habits prevent their
backs from returning to the condition that first brought them to
the chiropractor. It's hard for me to continue seeing the chiropractor
when I'm not in constant pain, but I know it's the only way to experience true healing and strength.

The worst thing you can do is go halfway and then quit.

We often neglect to continue healing journeys we've already
begun. I see this pattern repeated in many areas of life. We want

relief from the guilt that weighs us down, the difficulty of walking with the burden of a secret, or the pain of a life gone awry. Are we committed only to walking out of the darkness and getting relief, or will we commit to the process even when the pain is gone?

(
  "I AM VERY JUDGMENTAL."
)

SHORTCUTS

Our addiction to shortcuts makes strength training, whether physical, emotional, or spiritual, a really hard choice for us. We are quick to abandon the journey if we don't see the results. We all want the microwave option for freedom.

"Christians who let themselves be seduced into taking promised shortcuts of instant gratification that bypass the way of the Cross eventually find that the so-called gratifications turn into addictions, incapacitating them for mature relationships in household, workplace, and congregation," wrote Eugene Peterson.[25]

As a pastor I see this all the time. A guy who comes to me with tears in his eyes, a quivering lip, and urgency in his voice: "I need help. I am stuck in pornography. Tell me what to do. I will do whatever you tell me." They've experienced the pain of their sin and reached a breaking point.

I sit with these people, listen to their stories, pray with them, give them some instructions, and start them on the journey toward freedom. As I interact with them in the following weeks, they love walking in the light. The light is warm, refreshing, and freeing … and so much better than the darkness. As they experience the light, they begin to get comfortable with the relief they encounter. They no longer feel like they're standing on the brink of disaster, the urgent need for help has diminished, and things feel okay again. Fast-forward a few months, and they're no longer interested in the work needed to develop strength, or in staying on the path to freedom.

But the fact is that there are no shortcuts on this road.

(**"I CRAVE APPRECIATION AND RECOGNITION."**)

SPACE

While we must walk out of the darkness to experience freedom, it requires more to *live* in the light of freedom. We must develop the habits, disciplines, strength, and heart postures that cultivate a lifestyle of *light-living*. This process is about much more than exposing our secrets. If the process was only about exposure, we'd simply develop new secrets as soon as we confessed the old ones. This journey is about living a secret-free life that alters us at our core.

Changing the core of who we are and how we live is part of the journey. It requires great effort on our parts. This isn't the self-help effort we talked about avoiding in the last chapter; rather this effort goes toward whatever action will bring us in line with the Holy

Spirit's work. These disciplines connect us with His work of making us more like Jesus.

Trying to help ourselves leaves no space for God. Effort that cooperates with the work of God makes space for Him. Consider the ideas in part 1 of this book: the *actions* of confession and repentance. Repentance is not an effort that earns us salvation; it's an action that provides space for God and "*leads* to salvation" (2 Cor. 7:10). Repentance demands room in my life for God to work. Repentance is a prerequisite for receiving the grace of God.

Making that space doesn't just happen though. It requires intentionality in our thinking and spiritual discipline. This intentional effort is about *remaking*. It's about remaking our thought lives, remaking our heart postures, remaking our attitudes, and remaking our understandings of the community of faith. Ultimately it is about the deep remaking that can only come from God.

My prayer is that you will contribute to the process of remaking yourself and partner with the Holy Spirit so you can know firsthand what it means to walk in the light.

(**"I AM TERRIFIED TO HAVE ANOTHER BABY."**)

UNDERSTAND THE CONSEQUENCES

The work that needs to go on in our hearts is the formation of godly character. This character will be an internal compass tuned to the ways of God. This compass will lead us toward wisdom and away from immaturity and actions that will destroy our souls and relationships.

"Learning to navigate this world wisely, and to grow toward complete and mature human life in and though it all, is the challenge we all face," wrote N. T. Wright.[26] Character takes time to develop, so reminders of a life of weak character can be helpful.

(**"EVERY TIME I LOOK IN THE MIRROR I SEE MYSELF AS UGLY."**)

Our actions have consequences. The seeds we plant in our lives will produce fruit and have an impact on those around us. If I live a faithful, God-honoring life, not only will I personally experience the fruit of that obedience, but my family, friends, and colleagues will also be impacted in positive ways. Conversely, if I don't walk out of the darkness, and instead choose to guard my secrets, the consequences of my actions will injure me and ripple out to those I love as well.

With this in mind, I wrote a list in the back of my Bible. This list outlines the consequences of my sin if I were to blow it big time. I review the list often, and it serves as motivation for me to create space and regularly engage light-living. Here's my list:

I would grieve God. Ephesians 4:30 exhorts us, "Do not grieve the Holy Spirit of God." God is full of grace and forgiveness, but we know that He is also a father. As a father myself, I know that when my boys mess up, I grieve over their actions. I still love them dearly and accept them unconditionally, but I'm sad for what they've done to themselves, the consequences they will face, the people they affected, and the way they've represented the Stern family. Though our actions don't change our standing with God or how He views us, the greatest consequence of my sin is what it says to God.

(**"I WONDER IF I WILL EVER RECOGNIZE TRUE LOVE OR IF I WILL BE SCARED BY MY PARENTS' RELATIONSHIP."**)

I would face judgment from God. As a pastor and teacher, I know that the Bible says I will experience a more severe judgment than non-teachers (James 3:1). All Christians are accountable to God for their actions, but those who have spiritual authority in the lives of others are also accountable for how they have taught, led, and modeled. God has entrusted me to pastor thousands of college students and twentysomethings at theMILL—a responsibility I don't take lightly, nor would I look forward to the judgment that would come along with violating this trust.

I would bring shame and embarrassment on my wife. Though my sin would cost me personally, it would cost my wife dearly. If I were to blow it big, my sin would force my wife to live under a cloud of embarrassment and pay an extremely high price for my betrayal. Her trust in me would be shattered, the understanding of our relationship would crumble, and no matter how we repaired our relationship, things would never be the same.

I would heap pain on my boys. Exodus 34:7 states that actions of a father can carry on for generations. I'm not an expert on generational curses, but I do understand familial consequences. I have experienced the pain of self-centered parental choices, and I see it almost every day in others. One of the biggest responsibilities I have to my boys is to prepare them practically and spiritually for life. What I do as a father has an incredible impact on their future. They might experience the consequences of my sin by having to endure the pain of abandonment, the hurt of broken trust, and the destruction of their understanding of God as Father. I believe that as their earthly dad I am a part of shaping their understanding of their heavenly Father. I want them to see God as a Father who is good, trustworthy, and self-sacrificing.

(**"I AM ANGRY ALL THE TIME."**)

I would lose and disrupt friendships. No matter how close our friendships are, it's naive to think that they are exempt from the effects of our sin. All relationships are built on trust, and sin will destroy all that has been established. Some friends will be unable to trust again, and others will take time to come around.

It might be easy to say, "Well, I guess they weren't true friends in the first place." But the right response is to realize that the responsibility would fall directly on my shoulders.

I would violate those I lead. The Scriptures are clear that spiritual leaders should have a track record of faithful living (1 Tim. 3;

Titus 1). This is necessary to ensure the character of a leader and minimize the possibility of a double life, because the impact of a fallen leader on those they lead can be devastating. I don't ever want to face the overwhelming disappointment, contribute to a cloud of suspicion, or foster a low view of spiritual leaders among Christians and non-Christians.

I would undo a lot of hard work. I've worked really hard to be a good pastor. I've prayed with people, cried with people, laughed with people, and invested in people. I've walked with people through immense pain and loss, and have celebrated new birth in Christ and the live births of new babies. I would hate to have wasted all that effort and energy. I may even have to start over, unable to reap the benefits of my labors.

In the book of Proverbs, we find a warning against being seduced by the adulteress: "Do not go near the door of her house, lest you give your best strength to others and your years to one who is cruel, lest strangers feast on your wealth and your toil enrich another man's house" (Prov. 5:8–10). The benefits of years of faithful hard work can be thrown down the drain in a moment of passion and disappear forever.

I would undermine the work of the kingdom. God chose to build His church with people, and thankfully He is bigger than any sin we might commit. But this doesn't mean that our actions don't have an effect on the kingdom. The kingdom of God is evidenced by our submission to the rule of God in our lives. Sin is our statement that we have not fully submitted ourselves to the ways of God. As a leader in the kingdom, I want my life to communicate what kingdom living is all about—*not the opposite.*

Every time I ponder these horrific consequences, I actually get choked up. The thought of facing the people I care about the most and admitting to a violation of their trust is totally heartbreaking. The idea of facing my boys with an egregiously self-centered confession overwhelms my heart. I pray that this never happens, and I focus my energies toward developing the elements of character necessary to walk in and stay in the light.

(**"I NEED STRENGTH TO CONQUER MY DRUG ADDICTION. I AM DYING."**)

KRYPTONITE

When things are going well for us and we experience freedom, it's easy to develop a mind-set of invincibility. We begin to think that failure isn't even within the realm of possibility. First Corinthians 10:12 says, "If you think you are standing firm, be careful that you don't fall!" In Ephesians 6:11–14, Paul used the word *stand* four times to highlight the importance of keeping our feet under us.

No one, not me and not you, is ever immune to failure. I am nowhere near perfect, so I can't get lazy in keeping the habits of living in the light; primarily because I am *not* invincible. We are *all* susceptible. We all have the capability to cheat on our spouses, betray our colleagues, or steal something if the circumstances are right.

We may see someone blow it and think, *How could they? I would never do that.* While it may be true that you wouldn't fail in that particular way, I would bet that in the right situation you would blow it too. Proverbs 28:26 says, "He who trusts in himself is a fool, but he who walks in wisdom is kept safe." Living in the light requires that we develop a holy self-suspicion.

(**"SEX IS CONSUMING ME."**)

Superman can leap over buildings in a single bound, see through walls, and freeze objects with his breath, but he is never immune to kryptonite. He always has this major weakness before him. In the same way, we can live in the power of the Spirit, experience the redemption of God, and walk in the freedom found only in Jesus; and yet we are still not immune to falling.

The enemy is crafty and works to design a customized destruction plan for every one of us. The variety and depth of these plans is clearly reflected in the secrets displayed throughout this book. Please hear me in this: *To be self-suspicious is to resist giving yourself over to pride.* It is the presence of pride that sets us up for a fall (Prov. 16:18).

Therefore, we are not assuming we will fall, but we must be aware that we are not immune to falling. We are not invincible. It is this knowledge that will motivate us to continue the journey.

REFLECTION

/// Have you embraced any shortcuts in your journey toward freedom?

/// Write your own list of the consequences of your sins if you were to live a double life.

8

UNPACK YOUR BAGS

Josh has struggled with homosexual tendencies for as long as he can remember. He doesn't want to give into the temptations he experiences, but there is no part of him that likes the fight either. He hates it.

When he reads the words of Paul in Romans 7, "For what I want to do I do not do, but what I hate I do," Josh feels as if he is looking through a window into his own soul. He doesn't want the feelings he has. His knowledge of God's opinion concerning sexual sin and his desire for freedom are so strong that the continued struggle feels like failure. He often spirals into depression, disappointed with himself and angry with God.

I met Josh a couple of years ago, not long after he gave his life to Jesus. Realizing that his temptations didn't automatically subside after becoming a Christ follower, he found the courage to share his sin and overwhelming struggles with me. I thanked him for his openness and encouraged his desire to be free, telling him that freedom was possible. I shared that he was at a great starting point as he stepped out of the darkness and embraced the journey of confession. He shared his struggle with a few key people in his life and then came back to me and asked, "Now what?" We discussed the importance of repentance and renouncing sin, and then we talked about his past.

Josh doesn't know his dad. He never met him and doesn't even know if he's alive. At age six he gained a stepdad and a large extended family when his mom remarried. A lot more came with his new stepfamily than he guessed. Every time they had a family gathering, Josh was "touched" by his stepgrandfather and told to stay quiet about it.

In high school someone seduced and assaulted Josh in a public restroom. Someone later drugged and violated him at a party. These experiences ignited something in Josh. He began to explore the desires and longings he felt. Internet porn, masturbation, and sexual interchanges became commonplace. The past circumstances of Josh's life are tragic (although unfortunately common), but the big question is, what does he do with all this now?

Baggage like this—the hurts, memories, or habits that we carry with us—hinders us from experiencing freedom and healthy relationships. This baggage can consist of things we've done or things that have been done to us. Things we could control or things over which we had no control. Many of us are dragging around a U-Haul truck's worth of baggage. For Josh, moving forward with this weight around his heart was like trying to run while pulling a tractor trailer behind him.

If walking in the light means dragging around such an incredible weight in full view of everyone, then it's no wonder we think it's easier to stay in the dark and keep our baggage secret. However, if telling people about our baggage represents our first step out of the dark, the next step is to unload the trailer.

Josh needs to unpack his bags.

(**"I BLAME MY MOTHER FOR MY PARENTS'
DIVORCE AND HAVE NEVER FORGIVEN HER."**)

Feel Good

More than any other aspect of this journey, baggage unpacking is the place where people most often want a quick fix, frantically scurrying to find a shortcut. We ask, "Can't I skip this part? This is my past. *It's over.* I can't change anything, so why do I need to look at it?"

This line of thinking leads us to ask God to take away the struggle in a flash. Prayer is essential throughout our process, but the quick-fix prayer isn't where the answer lies. Walking in the light is about being willing to embrace the pain.

Naturally we don't like pain. This self-preservation translates into a dogged determination to avoid, downplay, and distance ourselves from any kind of pain, especially the dark pain of the past. We want things to be as convenient and comfortable as possible. Think about it: We live in a society where modern conveniences, technological advances, and medical breakthroughs give us the ability to relieve pain and discomfort quickly and with astounding regularity. If faced with a choice, we will choose the easier road 99.9 percent of the time. To voluntarily return to a painful time of our lives is counterintuitive and countercultural, not to mention grueling. We've trained our-selves to look for things that feel good and to believe that threats to our happiness are the enemy. This lie robs our lives of the richness that comes from pushing through pain and coming out the other side.

(**"I AM SELFISH WITH MY MONEY."**)

LOVE, HATE, AND A MOUNTAIN

Colorado Springs is an incredible place to live. The city is nestled up against the Rocky Mountains and sits at the base of Pikes Peak. The top of Pikes Peak stands 14,110 feet above sea level and is often cov-ered in snow into the middle of the summer. It really is spectacular and the sight of it causes Amos 4:13 to come alive: "He who forms the mountains, creates the wind, and reveals his thoughts to man, he who turns dawn to darkness, and treads the high places of the earth—the LORD God Almighty is his name." It's always a joy to see visitors standing in awe, staring at the mountains that I consider my backyard.

There are a few routes to the top of Pikes Peak. An old cog rail-way that is now reserved for tourists, a winding gravel road with no guardrails and several 1,000-foot drop-offs, and a couple of hiking trails, consisting of 13 miles and a serious lack of oxygen. I have hiked one of the trails a few times from bottom to top, and I have ridden my bike from top to bottom too. But there's another trail that I've hiked. This route cuts the total mileage from 13 to 10 by going straight up the mountain from the base. The first mile-long section of the path is what is called "the Incline."

Sounds like a nice weekly hike, doesn't it? Well, no. The Incline is brutal! The fastest I've ever ascended the trail is 33 minutes and 28 seconds. I have friends who can do the Incline in 25 minutes, and I know many others who land in the 40–50 minute range. No matter how you cut it, that's a pretty slow pace for a touch over a mile. And believe me, I'm not stopping to take in the view and smell the flowers. The Incline was originally a cable-car route. After a rockslide in 1990, the cable car and the tracks it ran on were removed, but the thick, wooden railroad ties were left behind. The railroad ties became the stairs that now make up the trail.

At its steepest point the Incline is a 68 percent grade, which causes me to hike using not just my feet but my hands as well. The trail climbs 2,011 feet in elevation—starting at about 6,574 feet above sea level. It is a StairMaster *on steroids*. If it isn't my legs that feel like jelly, then it's my lungs that feel like they're going to explode from a lack of oxygen. The *New York Times* ran a story about the Incline in 2008 and reported that it is used as a training regimen for Olympic athletes. The article quoted a wrestler saying the Incline counts among the most grueling workouts of his life. I am no Olympic athlete, but you get the point: *The Incline is not for the faint of heart.*

As I make my way to the start of the trail, I do a little stretching and set my watch to time my ascent. I feel pretty good about myself—I'm about to get some good exercise and enjoy the outdoors.

After pressing start on my stopwatch and heading up the mountain, it takes about five minutes for me to start feeling the burn. Five minutes later my body is telling me to stop, take a breather, and slow down. And five minutes after that I am tempted to sit down and soak in the view.

And am I ever tempted. During the rest of the hike I start questioning my sanity. *Why are you doing this? What were you thinking? You do know this is voluntary, right? No one is forcing you to do this, Aaron. You should turn around. What are you trying to prove? Stop! You are going to die!*

At this point I remind myself that the end is worth it, that the pain I am experiencing right now is a good pain, that my lungs and heart are not going to explode, and that I am not about to die. I've actually memorized several passages of Scripture that remind me of the value of pain and why I'm hiking the Incline. Why I shouldn't stop and why I really do want to push through to the finish:

> Since Jesus went through everything you're going through and more, learn to think like him. Think of your sufferings as a weaning from that old sinful habit of always expecting to get your own way. Then you'll be able to live out your days free to pursue what God wants instead of being tyrannized by what you want. (1 Peter 4:1–2 MSG)

> Do you not know that in a race all the runners run, but only one gets the prize? Run in such a

way as to get the prize. Everyone who competes in the games goes into strict training. They do it to get a crown that will not last; but we do it to get a crown that will last forever. Therefore I do not run like a man running aimlessly; I do not fight like a man beating the air. No, I beat my body and make it my slave so that after I have preached to others, I myself will not be disqualified for the prize. (1 Cor. 9:24–27)

Let us fix our eyes on Jesus, the author and perfecter of our faith, who for the joy set before him endured the cross, scorning its shame, and sat down at the right hand of the throne of God. Consider him who endured such opposition from sinful men, so that you will not grow weary and lose heart. (Heb. 12:2–3)

I suffer voluntarily on the Incline because I look at it as more than valuable physical exercise; it's also a huge benefit to my soul. When I tell my body to press on, when everything inside of me says to stop, turn around, or quit, I'm developing strength that I draw upon when I encounter other types of pain in life. When I unearth my past or bad habits that are difficult to untangle, I can take the long, strenuous, and sometimes overwhelming journey to the other side.

Making it even more difficult to hike the Incline is the trail to the bottom that veers off at the halfway point. This shortcut is so tempting. When I see it, I immediately think, *You've worked hard already. You can feel good about yourself if you stop now. Enjoy the shortcut!*

Isn't that how it is when we are in the middle of a painful journey? What appears to be a shortcut shows up at just the right time. We rationalize: *You've gone through enough pain. The benefit you've received so far is enough. Stop here.* Similarly, if we don't recognize the value of finishing the journey, it may take only a small temptation to convince us to stop pushing through the pain of working through our past.

(
    "I WANT SOMETHING I CAN'T HAVE."
)

I am motivated to push through the pains of life when I think about what it's like to make it to the top of the Incline. *The feeling is glorious.* No matter how long it takes to reach the top, the sense of accomplishment is incomparable. While the agonizing, questioning, and rationalizing are fresh and raw, the sensation of overcoming the challenge is palpable.

I love the Incline—it's a good workout, and I get to be outside and enjoy God's creation at the top. I also hate the Incline—the pain and energy required, the reality of my desire to quit at the middle.

We have a similar love/hate relationship with unpacking our bags. The idea of unpacking is a great one. Sifting through our history, looking for the walls we've built, uncovering our defense mechanisms, and discovering how we've fostered unforgiveness. Untangling all of this and walking in health and freedom—*I love it.* The fear, pain, effort, and time required to revisit the depth of our betrayals, disappointments, and violations—*I hate it.*

It's important to press through even when that love/hate tension is present. If we push through this, we will reach the top.

WE ALL HAVE IT

No one is exempt. We all carry baggage. Some of it is good and some of it isn't.

Maybe the bags you carry involve your family history. The abandonment of a father, the neglect of a mother, or the way a sibling treated you. Maybe one is a bag of hurtful words that someone said about you—*loser, worthless,* or *unwanted.* Or one could be the words that were *never* said—*I love you, I want to be with you,* or *you are valuable.* Maybe another is a past relationship. Even though the relationship ended long ago, perhaps you carry it with you wherever you go, including every new relationship. Maybe the feeling of rejection lives on inside you even today.

And if you think you don't have any baggage, well, you might want to consider the bag of pride—the one that causes you to think you don't have any bags.

As a pastor who works with a lot of people every day, I am both sad and intrigued when I see patterns of alcoholism or abuse passed down from one generation to another. At first glance that sounds ridiculous. Surely those who've experienced the fallout of alcoholism or abuse firsthand would be the last ones to participate in such patterns themselves. However, the baggage handed down by an alcoholic or abusive parent or relative doesn't go away; instead it evolves and reproduces, propelling the children toward a similar course.

This process happens to any bag. A bag of rejection develops a defense mechanism that rejects others before they can reject you. The bag of neglect by a father drives you to find love in the arms of any man who will have you. Or the bag of hurtful words and verbal abuse creates a new bag of aggression, defensiveness, and isolation. The bags get bigger, multiplying and growing—all while undermining everything you desperately want and need.

The most common response is to pack up our bags, put some locks on them, and drop them in a dark corner. We think, *What I ignore will go away.* This strategy couldn't be more wrong.

(**"I HAVE BECOME INDIFFERENT TO SIN."**)

Have you ever tried to swim with a beach ball under your stomach? It can be done for a little while, but you'll often swim in circles and eventually the ball will pop out from under the water. That's what it's like to leave your baggage unattended, hoping it will magically disappear. It's possible to hide baggage for a little while, but eventually it will shoot out sideways and explode into your life.

Just so you know, we never totally eliminate our baggage. But we can minimize it and keep it from becoming a burden. The goal is to downsize from a U-Haul to something more manageable. Our goal is to keep baggage from taking up so much space in our hearts and heads that we can't see straight.

RESPONSIBILITY

"Aaron, you just don't understand. If you knew what happened to me, you would realize that I'm not to blame." I hear something like this on a pretty regular basis. "My parents, my boyfriend, my friend, my teacher, or my pastor did this." Or maybe it's God who gets the blame. "I was dealt some terrible cards, so it's not my fault I have this baggage!"

Maybe, just like Josh, you were a victim. But there's a difference between being victimized and living in victimization.

It may seem obvious, but it must be said: *We are each responsible for our baggage.* Not that we are responsible to figure it all out—ultimately God brings freedom. Regardless of how we got the baggage in the first place, it's our responsibility to deal with it. We must be faithful and bring our hearts and all that lies within us to God. No one else will—and no one else can.

HOW?

So the million-dollar question is this: *How do I unpack my bags?* As you've read this book, I'm sure you've figured out by now that there isn't a simple formula and it's not all about you.

No matter what path you take, the most important step is to invite the work of the Holy Spirit. He guides us by revealing truth, convicting us of our sins, and comforting us (John 16:7–8, 12–13). Our natural tendency is to ignore our baggage, so we need the Holy

Spirit to guide us toward it, convict us, comfort us, and lead us toward truth as we unpack it.

(**"I AM AFRAID THAT MY FAITH WILL NEVER BE GOOD ENOUGH."**)

TRIGGERS

Sometimes it is easy to identify the baggage in our lives, but other times it can be tricky. I find it helpful to look for patterns. Try asking yourself the following questions:

What are the things I bump into over and over again? Is there an area of my life where I feel stuck? Do my relationships only seem to go to a certain point? Is there some pain that I am covering, maybe with food, work, sleep, porn, anger, etc.?

Answering these questions might not produce anything substantive, so I also encourage you to look for what I call *triggers*. Triggers are outward signs of something bigger going on under the surface. Do you ever respond to situations with a disproportionate amount of emotion?

During my summers as a teenager, I worked for my dad, who was a general contractor. In high school I didn't like getting up at six a.m. to dig foundations or trenches, insulate attics, or scrape weathered paint off houses—all while my friends got paid to get tans as lifeguards at the local pool or slept in until noon and then sold hotdogs at the AAA baseball stadium. As much as I hated it at the time, I'm grateful for the skills I learned. Now I actually enjoy working on my house, on my schedule. Home improvement has become a sort of therapeutic hobby for me. Sometimes when things are hectic, I look forward to the days when I can get out my toolbox and work with my hands as I do something that doesn't require a lot of thought.

I used those skills several years ago when I painted my house. My house was built in 1904, and trust me, old houses require a lot of TLC. I've filled many a weekend with demolition, landscaping, and trips to Home Depot.

One beautiful day, I was on the roof painting a second-story window when I saw my wife, Jossie, pull the car out of the garage. Unfortunately I'd left a five-gallon bucket of paint on the driveway, and she slammed the car right into it, spilling paint everywhere!

I practically jumped off the roof to assess the situation. As I got to the spill, I yelled at the top of my lungs, "Why is this happening? Can't anything go right?" Then I kicked the empty bucket and let out a few expletives.

(**"I HAVE ABUSED SOMEONE IN MY FAMILY."**)

After a significant cleanup operation, Jossie asked me about my reaction, recognizing that it wasn't normal behavior for me. "What happened out there today, Aaron? What was behind your explosive frustration? That is so unlike you."

Although the situation was definitely unfortunate, my response had been over the top. The spilled paint triggered something in me that had been bubbling below the surface for a while. As we talked about it, we identified several recent and hurtful events that had upset me. My reaction that day was in response to everything that had been going on, not just a painted-over driveway.

(**"I CAN'T FORGIVE MYSELF."**   )

Triggers in our lives are like indicator lights on a dashboard of a car: They signal the driver that something wrong is happening under the hood. Anger, depression, irritation, and laughing at a sad situation are lights on the dashboard of our hearts. When the Check Engine light goes on, the goal is not to turn off the light but to address the issue that caused the light to go on in the first place.

Covering the light with duct tape may get rid of the light, but the issue that caused the light still persists. Denial simply allows the initial problem to grow worse or create deeper problems while we ignore it. I have a friend who drove around ignoring a "funny noise" in her car for months and didn't take it to a shop until the car broke down on the side of the road and had to be towed. It turned out that the initial problem would have been a cheap fix, but ignoring the problem had created additional issues that cost her nearly $450!

Freedom isn't entirely about controlling external behavior. True freedom comes as we dig for what lies beneath and deal with the bigger problem so that it cannot control our actions anymore. This is the difference between *looking like we're free* and *actually being free.*

FRIENDS

Sometimes it can be difficult to see and identify your own issues. Often the most direct route to your baggage is to ask trusted friends to help you identify negative patterns or blind spots in your life. However, involving other people in the process might make this the scariest route as well.

I can hear your response now: "Whoa! Isn't it daunting enough to identify that I have a U-Haul full of baggage by myself? Why would I invite others into this process?"

Just as we need community when we come out of the darkness and confess what's in our hearts, we also need community as we walk in the light and sort through all the baggage we've been carrying around. Here are a couple questions you can ask your friends that will bring baggage to the surface:

> What is it that everybody knows but nobody says to me?
> What are a *couple* things (not *seventeen*) that keep me from healthy relationships?
> Describe what it's like to be my friend.

It's important that you let your friends know that you want them to be brutally honest with you and that you won't react with a "No

I'm not!" or a "Well then, let me tell you what everyone wants to say to you."

Take what they say to prayer and commit to trusting that they might be right. Remember, we never develop holistic maturity on our own. It always comes from a shared life with others in the faith.

(**"DECEPTION IS ONE OF MY BEST AND MOST HATED SKILLS."**)

HELP

I'm really only scratching the surface of how to unpack baggage. It truly is a necessary skill for life and something that may not come naturally for many. I encourage you to pick up other good books as additional resources to this book in dealing with the baggage that so easily piles up in our hearts. Some books that may be of help include Neil T. Anderson's *Victory Over the Darkness* and Henry Cloud and John Townsend's *How People Grow*.

There may be times in your own personal unpacking process that you get stuck. If you get to this point, I recommend spending time with a counselor. Before you say "No way, I don't need a shrink. Shrinks are for crazy people, and I am not crazy," I urge you to drop your preconceived ideas of what it means to see a counselor and who sees them. Counselors are really just professional baggage unpackers. They are trained to help people move through the history of their lives, deal with things appropriately, and develop healthy life patterns for the future.

All counselors are not equal, so I recommend you find the right one. First, look for a Christian counselor. The ultimate goal in this process is to engage God's grace, but a counselor who approaches the inner workings of your life without a biblical framework won't be able to help. And not all Christian counselors are equal, so take time to find someone with whom you feel comfortable. It might also be a good idea to meet with somebody who specializes in whatever area you are dealing with (sexual abuse, codependency, eating disorders, children of alcoholics, etc.). Seek recommendations from trusted friends or a pastor.

There is no shame in seeing a counselor. I have seen a counselor. My wife is a counselor and has seen a counselor herself as well. I recommend people to counselors on almost a weekly basis. They are often hesitant at first but will later report back to say that it is well worth the time and expense.

And remember John from chapter 7? He has been seeing a professional baggage unpacker himself to talk about his views of women and pornography. Here's what he has to say about the partnership in his journey:

I think counseling was crucial to my recovery because a professional is able to identify your problems, not address your symptoms. For years, I had been trying quick fixes like getting an Internet filter, or cancelling my cable … it's helpful but that's not a long-term solution. I'd see short stints of success but I'd eventually find new ways to meet my needs. Through counseling, I discovered that my real issues were unmet needs in childhood and anger I had carried with me because of a broken relationship with my parents. Alcoholism, drug addiction, workaholism … those are not problems; they are symptoms of problems. Pornography and masturbation was just the way I chose to medicate my real issues. Once I identified my real issues and worked through them, the pornography and masturbation just kinda became irrelevant, I no longer had the desires.

(**"I AM SO LONELY THAT I WOULD BE WILLING TO GO BACK INTO A PHYSICALLY ABUSIVE RELATIONSHIP SO SOMEONE SPENDS TIME WITH ME."**)

There is no shame in needing help. In fact, coming to the ends of ourselves and admitting that we need help are powerful acts of humility that give space for God to do a deep work in our hearts.

LONG ROAD

Unpacking your bags is a lifelong process. So dive in. God has freedom for you on the other side. Don't stop after unpacking one bag—*go for the next one!*

And even when the process of unpacking is arduous and long, remember: "He who began a good work in you will carry it on to completion" (Phil. 1:6).

REFLECTION

/// Can you identify any baggage you need to unpack?

If so, what?

/// What scares you about unpacking your baggage?

/// Do you need help to begin unpacking?

9

MAKING THINGS RIGHT

Whenever I travel, my goal is to fit everything into my carry-on luggage without having to check anything. I enjoy the ease of skipping baggage claim and having everything I need with me should an unforeseen circumstance present itself.

Recently I was unable to get a week's worth of clothes into a bag that would fit in the overhead compartment, so I reluctantly checked my bag. The airline attendant behind the desk said, "That will be twenty dollars. Would you like to pay for that with cash or credit?" Having gone without checking a bag for several years, I found this new fee to be an unpleasant surprise.

As I stood there, I began to wonder if there was a way to offload some things so I wouldn't have to check my bag. For this particular trip I had packed two extra pairs of shoes, which I figured were the culprits for making my bag too large for a carry-on. So essentially I was paying twenty dollars just to bring my shoes along!

Just as offloading some bags before going to the airport saves money, offloading baggage in your life saves you from the pain and difficulty of bearing unnecessary weight. And forgiveness is one of the best ways to unload some significant baggage.

(**"I FOOLED AROUND WITH A VERY UNDERAGE GIRL. I'VE NEVER EVEN TOLD GOD."**)

MAMA DRAMA

In the years after high school I realized I carried some bags wearing the label "Mom." I had a good share of what I like to call "mama drama," something that people who carry a mom bag often encounter.

My mom was a good mother to me when I was growing up. She made great meals, drove me to my soccer games, made my friends feel welcome at our house, and created a nice home environment for my siblings and me. However, in high school I became aware of some serious difficulties in my parents' relationship, which later led to their divorce. My parents' divorce sent shockwaves through our family, creating a fissure between my mom and me. We experienced misunderstandings, unmet expectations, and wrong assumptions, all of which led to hurts, bitterness, and eventually, a distance that permeated our relationship for years. As I grew up, I found myself extremely disappointed, mad, and hungry for justice.

I expressed these deep hurts, not only in my relationship with my mom, but also in unhealthy relational habits with others. My mom bag grew larger and eventually leaked into other areas of my life.

Although we're eager to feel better, I think many of us often fixate on things outside of our control in situations like this. Deep inside, I wanted my mom to acknowledge how she had hurt me, to apologize, and to change the way she interacted with me. But this was the wrong place for me to start. I had to start in the only place I had any control: *my own heart.*

(**"I'M MAD ABOUT THE WAY GOD MADE ME."**)

LET GO

The fastest way to clean out your heart is simply to forgive. I know that this is much easier said than done, but it's true. Emphasizing the destructive nature of not forgiving someone, Hebrews 12:14–15 encourages us to forgive liberally:

> Make every effort to live in peace with all men and
> to be holy; without holiness no one will see the
> Lord. See to it that no one misses the grace of God
> and that no bitter root grows up to cause trouble
> and defile many.

The word *forgive* literally means "to release, to let go of." In the New Testament, the writers use the word *forgiveness* to describe releasing someone from a financial obligation. So if you were to release someone from a debt, you would say, "You don't owe me anything." Similarly, to release someone from a hurt they caused you, you would say, "I am not holding on to what you did to me. You don't owe me anything."

(**"I'M SO DESPERATE TO ESCAPE FROM THE GUILT AND PRISON THAT FOOD HAS CREATED."**)

I had to forgive my mom and let go of things that I held onto in my heart. I needed to get to the place in my heart where I could say, "You don't owe me." I struggled with this because my interactions with my mom were difficult, which just piled new hurts on to old hurts. I thought I could forgive her so long as she would stop hurting me.

How often are we like that?

We justify our failure to forgive because our situation is "unique." I've heard all the excuses about why forgiveness isn't possible; however, we must remember the words of Jesus as He interacted with Peter:

> Then Peter came to Jesus and asked, "Lord, how many times shall I forgive my brother when he sins against me? Up to seven times?" Jesus answered, "I tell you, not seven times, but seventy-seven times." (Matt. 18:21–22)

Maybe Jesus said this knowing that our tendency is to talk ourselves out of forgiving. We always have a good reason why we're exempt from this commandment after people hurt us repeatedly. But there is no biblical caveat that says, "Forgive unless you can't muster up the strength or unless your situation is really, really bad."

There is no disclaimer. Forgiveness is a must.

Matthew 6:14–15 is a powerful reminder of how quickly we forget God's forgiveness for our own wretched sinfulness. Our excuses pale in comparison to that for which we have been forgiven. It should be great motivation to forgive: "For if you forgive men when they sin against you, your heavenly Father will also forgive you. But if you do not forgive men their sins, your Father will not forgive your sins."

It is in the act of setting others free that we can be set free ourselves.

("I WAS RAPED.")

WHEN YOU CAN'T DO IT

Although I've forgiven others for varying degrees of violation, I may not feel warm, fuzzy feelings toward them afterward. My goal is to release my negative emotions to God; sometimes this is a monthly exercise, though other times it seems like a never-ending cycle. Forgiveness does not mean that you forget; it means that you let go of your anger, bitterness, and desire for revenge. Instead you love your enemies and pray for those who persecute you. But obviously this does require supernatural empowerment.

I've heard horrific stories of how people have been violated and traumatized. When I suggest that they need to forgive the one who hurt them, initially it might seem incomprehensible, even impossible. And I think it is ... *on our own*. That is why we must rely on the Holy Spirit to empower us to forgive.

After the conclusion of a long murder trial, I heard on the news the mother of the slain daughter boldly state, "I will never forgive!" In earthly terms this made a lot of sense to me, but in kingdom terms this makes no sense at all. We are called to forgive; and we must forgive, no matter what the offense.

("I WAS SEXUALLY ABUSED BY MY GRANDPA. I HAVE ANGER BECAUSE MY FAMILY DIDN'T PROTECT ME.")

WHAT IT IS NOT

So if we know that the Bible says clearly that we are to forgive, why don't we do it?

In our culture of self-service and feel-good everything, the way of forgiveness is entirely countercultural. Based on conversations with many people, I think this often stems from what we think forgiveness means. I find it helpful to talk with people about what forgiveness *is not*.

Forgiveness is not about removing the pain. The pain of the offense can be acute and serve as a reminder of the wound. We often want the pain to go away before we'll forgive the offender. We must work through the pain, but this can't be an excuse to hold back forgiveness. Forgiveness is a statement made from a place of truth; unforgiveness is a statement made from an emotional place.

"I OVEREAT."

Forgiveness is not about discounting the pain. The pain of a violation can be real and overwhelming. Remember, forgiving an offense is not a statement about the pain but a statement about how you will respond to the pain.

Forgiveness is not an attempt to remove the significance of the event. Have you ever had someone apologize for hurting you and your response was a quick "It's not a big deal" or "It was nothing" when really it was huge? Their hurtful words or thoughtlessness crushed you, and yet you blew it off as nothing. Forgiveness is not about communicating that the violation you experienced "was nothing." Even though you forgive someone, it doesn't mean that the pain is irrelevant. Forgiveness is a statement about your heart, not about the significance of the event.

Forgiveness is not about forgetting. God is the One who forgives and forgets (Heb. 8:12). Someone may try to forgive and yet remember the pain. Some believe that because they haven't forgotten that they haven't yet forgiven. Forgiveness is not a statement about the existence of a memory but a statement about how we remember.

Forgiveness is not dependent on an apology or a request for forgiveness. Forgiveness would be so much easier if the offender saw the pain he or she caused, apologized, and asked for forgiveness. It would be easier if the person changed his or her behavior and somehow paid for the damage that the offense caused. Just as Jesus forgave the thief on the cross, we must not set these conditions for someone to "earn" our forgiveness. Forgiveness is a free gift to us from God, and it's the same when we offer it to those who have wronged us. Forgiveness is not a statement about the offender being "worth" forgiving; rather it's a statement that all can be forgiven.

Forgiveness is not about the other person being right. To say "I forgive you" does not mean "You were right, I was wrong." You aren't releasing others from responsibility or consequences when you forgive. However, you do release them from taking up residence in your heart. Forgiveness is not a statement about right and wrong but a statement of release and surrender.

Forgiveness is not about disregarding justice. For me, holding on to an offense reflects my desire for the offender to hurt as much as I have. We don't like to be this honest, but our hesitance to forgive is often based in our desire for some kind of revenge. However, it's not our place to see that others pay for their actions; that job belongs to God. Forgiveness is not a statement about disregarding justice but a statement about who will execute justice.

"I'VE BEEN TO A STRIP CLUB."

REVENGE

When we aren't willing to forgive, we communicate that we're not dependent on God. To forgive is to release others, to say that they owe us nothing, and to give up our desire to enact revenge. Romans 12:19 says, "Don't insist on getting even; that's not for you to do. 'I'll do the judging,' says God. 'I'll take care of it'" (MSG).

For some reason we think that we're hurting others by holding on to the offense, but in reality we are just hurting ourselves. I've heard it said that "holding on to bitterness and resentment is like taking poison and waiting for the other person to die."

Forgiveness is currency in the kingdom of God because it's about surrendering to God's ways and giving Him space in our hearts. Ultimately the act of forgiveness trusts God to take care of us and to execute justice on our behalf.

> "MY SISTER GOT PREGNANT AT 17 AND IT CHANGED OUR FAMILY. SINCE THEN I'VE BLAMED HER CHILD FOR MESSING UP OUR FAMILY."

JUSTICE HAS BEGUN

Jesus is a perfect example of showing us how to trust God's justice. "When they hurled their insults at him, he did not retaliate; when he suffered, he made no threats. Instead, he entrusted himself to him who judges justly" (1 Peter 2:23).

Jesus, being God, had the ability to retaliate in a big way. He could have called on all the angels of heaven to rescue Him, struck the soldiers who beat Him with lightning, or transported Himself to another place. Yet He entrusted Himself to His Father and His justice. He knew that His Father would carry out justice.

(**"I AM AFRAID THAT IF PEOPLE KNOW THAT I HAVE FAILED THEY WILL NOT LOVE ME ANYMORE."**)

Our culture embraces a kind of wrath that exercises vigilante justice, but Jesus said that God is just, meaning that perfect justice will happen in His perfect timing. And Jesus' death clearly rejected wrath, revenge, and any kind of unforgiveness. As children of God we must follow the model of Jesus and respond with an active trust in the justice of God.

It can be difficult to trust that God works on our behalf because we rarely see something happen right away. We want to see the offender suffer immediately (and maybe for a long time). But the reality is that God desires the elimination of evil and injustice even more than we do. So much so that He did something about it!

When we turn to bitterness or wrath, failing to forgive, we become part of the problem. Our humanity broke things in the first place, so why do we think our own fix will contribute to true justice? Do we really believe that getting even will make the world right?

When Jesus died on the cross, He took on the weight of sin and evil, and in resurrection His kingdom burst forth. Jesus talked about the kingdom more than any other subject during His earthly ministry. The kingdom of God is not about political dominance but about remaking the world and rescuing the cosmos. God's plan all along was to take the brokenness of the world and make it right. (For a more detailed explanation of the kingdom and God's rescue plan, read Glenn Packiam's *Lucky* or N. T. Wright's *Simply Christian*.) As followers of Jesus we join God and His kingdom, and so by forgiving those who have violated us, we use the currency of the kingdom and bring forth the remaking plan of God.

However, sometimes we get impatient when we don't see the kingdom working and the immediate righting of all wrongs. The fact is that God's perfect kingdom has only begun and we haven't experienced it in its fullness. So we must live in the tension of knowing that God's perfect work has begun but is not yet finished. Justice has begun, and God will finish it.

It is for this reason that Paul could say from a Roman prison in Philippians 1:19: "For I know that through your prayers and the help given by the Spirit of Jesus Christ, what has happened to me will turn out for my deliverance."

Paul didn't know he would be freed at this point—all he knew was that he would be executed the next day. The word *deliverance* used by Paul is the Greek word *soteria,* which means *salvation.* He wasn't talking about having a guarantee of physical deliverance from prison; he was writing about his ultimate salvation. He knew that he was part of the global rescue plan of God. For Paul, justice had begun.

(**"I AM FILLED WITH SO MUCH ANGER AND RAGE."**)

BEST

So if feelings, forgetfulness, change, or apologies are not conditions for forgiveness, how do we know if we have forgiven someone? Is it a matter of saying the right words and being done with it? In my experience, and as indicated by Jesus in Matthew 18, forgiveness is an ongoing process. Does that mean we don't ever really get over it? No. It means that we must have a realistic idea of what it means to forgive.

You will know you've fully forgiven someone when you begin to want the best for him or her. That doesn't mean that you're hoping for that person's earthly success; rather you hope for God's best in his or her life. You want peace and life and truth and wholeness to reign.

If you find this impossible, you might take a look at the posture of your heart. Tim Keller once said, "It is impossible to forgive someone if you feel superior to him or her."[27] It's tempting to think that because that person did something you would *never* do, that somehow you're a better person. This self-righteousness can keep our hearts locked up with bitterness and unnecessary baggage.

If you choose not to forgive, you will be the one who suffers. In the end, those you don't forgive will hold you hostage—not the other way around.

("I SWEAR ALL THE TIME. IN TRUTH—I LOVE SWEARING."   )

Do I Really Want To?

After many years of tension, distance, and mama drama, I didn't think there was hope for a healthy relationship with my mom. I'd forgiven her and concluded that she didn't owe me anything. I really wanted God's best for her and was settled into what our relationship may look like for years to come.

But then, out of the blue, things came to a head. It started via email, and after a few heated exchanges, my mom suggested we sit down and talk. I agreed to meet her with one condition: In order for us to move forward, we first would need to address the past, acknowledge hurts, and accept responsibility. She agreed, and our first date was set.

("I don't care about anyone around me.")

The conversation started off bumpy, but as we talked, lights came on for my mom, and she gained a new awareness of the pain she'd caused. And I realized times when I hadn't been gracious toward her. Tears flowed as we discussed previously off-limits topics. We talked about rejection, dysfunction, family history, divorce, and our perceptions. At times it felt surreal—I sat there in a minor state of shock. I pinched myself to make sure I wasn't dreaming. Then came the words that could change everything:

"Will you forgive me?"

I wasn't prepared for this. I knew that my response to this question was not one to be taken lightly. If I said yes, it would mean something for our relationship. Not just a release in my heart, but it would mean the beginning of a new relationship.

My response wasn't immediate, though I knew what I was supposed to do.

I actually kinda like being mad at you, I thought. *I don't remember what it's like not to carry hurt and disappointment about you. I have held on to this for a long time now. Do I really want this to change?*

I didn't know who I would be without that baggage—like it or not, it had become part of who I was. I would have to adjust to the weight change. The tricks to carrying the weight would become useless. *This was big.*

The reality is that most people are deeply connected to their hurt. It becomes part of their identities. To let go of it means major change.

("MY HUSBAND IS ADDICTED TO INTERNET PORN AND I THINK IT'S MY FAULT BECAUSE I'M UGLY.")

TRUST

Forgiveness is based on grace. It isn't earned, deserved, or asked for. It's a posture of our hearts; it's a command from Jesus and the way of the kingdom. The question my mom asked was a different question. The answer she sought had to do with trust.

This is the reason that when we forgive someone it doesn't mean that everything goes back to "normal." In his book *Exclusion and*

Embrace, Yale professor and leading theologian Miroslav Volf said that wrongs must be identified, named, and dealt with before parties can find reconciliation.[28] And if someone violates and hurts us repeatedly, we would be unwise to trust them as before. Boundaries are necessary for the protection of our hearts and health. If every time I walked around a certain corner I got hit in the head by a guy swinging a baseball bat, it would be stupid for me not to find a new route—or at least not to duck if I had to go around that corner again.

The forgiveness we extend to others is really an experience in grace and has to do with our relationship with God. The forgiveness we extend to others in reconciliation is an experience in trust and has to do with our relationships with other people. Grace is free, while trust is earned. One is vertical and the other is horizontal.

I said yes to my mom's request and asked for forgiveness for the ways I had contributed to our relational difficulties. She also said yes. Since then things have improved dramatically. Our relationship didn't heal overnight, but we're rebuilding trust over time, and reconciliation is happening.

("SOMETIMES I DON'T EAT BECAUSE I'M SCARED I'LL GAIN TOO MUCH WEIGHT.")

I'm grateful for the miracle that occurred in my relationship with my mom. Now we're on course for a healthy, mature, and loving relationship. Had there been no change after our conversation, reconciliation would have come to a screeching halt, but the requirement for forgiveness in my heart would have been the same.

Forgiveness is not synonymous with trust. Our relationship with God is built on grace, and our relationships with others are built on trust; and when that trust is violated, it changes the dynamic of the relationship. Though you may forgive the person relatively quickly, trust is built over time. Forgiveness is a prerequisite for trust, but trust does not automatically follow forgiveness. Depending on the violation, trust may never fully return.

I think of it like filling a bathtub with water. Building trust is similar to filling the tub with a drip or slow trickle; it will fill up in time. When someone damages that trust, especially in a significant way, it's like pulling the plug and draining the water quickly. Refilling the tub again will take time. If the person demonstrates trustworthiness over time, the tub can be refilled and trust can be reestablished.

(**"I FEEL LIKE GOD FORGOT TO GIVE ME A PURPOSE."**)

BE THE FIRST

Forgiveness can be a tough issue, so I encourage you to determine ahead of time how you will respond to offenses. Make a decision that you will forgive no matter how painful, deep, or common the hurts.

Determine that you will be a person who extends grace to others just as God did to us.

(**"I CHEATED ON ALMOST ALL MY EXAMS IN COLLEGE."**)

In hurtful situations we can spend energy trying to get the other person to ask for forgiveness. I've found that the fastest way to see someone else ask you for forgiveness (though never a guarantee) is to ask for forgiveness yourself first. You might be responsible for only 1 percent of the problem, but take ownership of that and ask for forgiveness.

Be the first.

God calls us to live forward-looking lives and not to live in the past. As we live this way, we can feel the baggage of our hearts get lighter and see His kingdom come into our lives.

REFLECTION

/// Is there anyone whom you haven't forgiven?

/// What makes forgiveness difficult for you?

/// Pray God's best for those who have hurt you.

/// Is there anything you can do to reconcile with someone and begin to build trust again?

10

HOOKS AND LIES

Interstate 25 runs north and south through Colorado Springs, and I drive this bustling six-lane thoroughfare to work every day. It's the first road to get snow plowed in the winter, is regularly locked up during rush hour, and is frequently monitored for commuters on the local radio stations.

To help drivers better anticipate and navigate what might be ahead, the authorities installed massive jumbotron-sized screens every few miles to communicate with drivers. They're often used for notifications of upcoming crashes, icy roads, AMBER Alerts, or information about road-construction schedules.

("IN THE PAST 3 MONTHS I HAVE TRIED TO KILL MYSELF TWICE. TONIGHT IT WAS MY PLAN TO FINISH THE JOB.")

One summer morning I was driving north to my office and saw the following message blitzing across the screens:

"SPEED TRAP AHEAD. PLEASE DRIVE THE SPEED LIMIT."

That's interesting, I thought. The message seemed counterintuitive to me. If they really wanted to trap speeders the police certainly wouldn't tell people what they were doing. They'd hide in the bushes and pounce when we least expected it.

Sure enough, not far down the road I saw an army of motorcycle police lined up on the side of the freeway with speed-tracking guns drawn. But what I found amazing was what I saw another mile down the road: a long line of cars pulled over by policemen, receiving speeding tickets.

Who are these people? Did they not see the message? Or did they simply not believe the message on the screen? The local news reported later that week that a record had been set in the number of people pulled over for speeding on I-25.

That is incredible! The warning was out in the open, and yet people didn't respond to it. It's one thing not to know what to expect and get caught off guard—it's a whole different story when the road ahead is clearly described for us.

I wonder how much we're like this every day. We move through life wanting to live in a place of safety, joy, and freedom. And yet we often ignore the signs that tell us exactly what is up ahead and how to avoid the ditch of pain and bondage. What if we knew what to expect? What if we could clearly see the strategy the enemy plans to use against us? (Oh, and please don't think I'm comparing the police force to Satan by the way, as I greatly appreciate all our law enforcement men and women do for us.)

The truth is, the thousands of years of history recorded in the Scriptures give us, with striking clarity, Satan's basic plan of attack. I pray that we heed the warning and live accordingly rather than drive on by oblivious.

("ON THE OUTSIDE I TREAT WOMEN WITH RESPECT BUT ON THE INSIDE I AM FULL OF LUST.")

NO MORE MR. NICE GUY

To best understand Satan's strategy, it is crucial that we know his goal. He's not trying to just bully us or play pranks—he's trying to kill us, steal from us, and ultimately destroy us (John 10:10). The Bible says that Satan is the enemy of our souls, and Peter encouraged us to "be sober-minded; be watchful. Your adversary the devil prowls around like a roaring lion, seeking someone to devour" (1 Peter 5:8 ESV). The Devil is the enemy, and he's not just trying to knock you down; he's trying to take you out. And he will do whatever it takes.

Ephesians 6:10–12 communicates how we should interact with the enemy:

> Be strong in the Lord and in his mighty power. Put on the full armor of God so that you can take your stand against the devil's schemes. For our struggle is not against flesh and blood, but against the rulers, against the authorities, against the powers of this dark world and against the spiritual forces of evil in the heavenly realms.

We are in a struggle of cosmic proportions that we should take very seriously. I love how *The Message* Bible translates this passage:

> God is strong, and he wants you strong. So take everything the Master has set out for you, well-made weapons of the best materials. And put them to use so you will be able to stand up to everything the Devil throws your way. This is no afternoon athletic contest that we'll walk away from and forget about in a couple of hours. This is for keeps, a life-or-death fight to the finish against the Devil and all his angels.

The Devil isn't playing around. He's planning our demise, so it's vital that we know his strategy and live in such a way that will counter his desires for us.

(**"I CONSTANTLY COMPARE MYSELF TO OTHERS AROUND ME."**)

CONSISTENT

You might be thinking, *Wait, I haven't seen any jumbotron signs warning me of the schemes of the enemy on the road ahead.* But as we look at the Scriptures, we see thousands of years of history and get to observe the ways the Devil works against God and His people.

We can clearly see the patterns, and vivid pictures of his schemes emerge.

(**"I HAVEN'T TALKED TO MY SON IN OVER A YEAR. HE IS FOUR AND A HALF."**)

We first see Satan in the garden of Eden in Genesis 3 when he immediately reveals his goals with the first words out of his mouth: "Did God really say …" (Gen. 3:1). He goes on to tempt and deceive Eve to believe that God isn't who He says He is.

Satan regularly attempts and often succeeds to lead the people of God astray throughout the Old Testament by getting them to believe that God is not enough for them. He convinces people of their need to embrace other gods for fulfillment, security, or peace. Over and over again, they break their covenants with God and believe that He isn't worth their wholehearted devotion.

Satan's attempts to draw people away from God persist in the New Testament as well. He continues by trying to deceive the Son of God. When Jesus is in the desert, the Devil attempts to warp the words of God (as if Jesus didn't know what God had said) and tempt Jesus to take things into His own hands.

Paul highlighted Satan's persistent attempts to destroy the church. He worried that we will "somehow be led astray from [our] sincere and pure devotion to Christ" (2 Cor. 11:3). False teachers threatened the Corinthian church by preaching a different gospel (2 Cor. 11:4), the Galatians were tempted to indulge their sinful nature (Gal. 5:13), and the church at Colossae sometimes depended on human reasoning and philosophy (Col. 2:8).

(**"I BETRAYED ONE OF MY BEST FRIENDS."**)

The Devil is a liar, and he attempts to do the same thing to you that he's done throughout the ages. He wants you to believe his lies like Eve did in the garden. He is cunning, crafty, and he is trying to lead us away from Jesus. His tactic reflects the meaning of his name: *deceiver.*

John 8:44 says, "[Satan] was a murderer from the beginning, not holding to the truth, for there is no truth in him. When he lies, he speaks his native language, for he is a liar and the father of lies." Again, the apostle John stated in Revelation 12:9 that "the great dragon was hurled down—that ancient serpent called the devil, or Satan, who leads the whole world astray."

He is a liar by nature, and his deception usually sounds something like this:

"Just try it once."

"It isn't that big of a deal."

"God will forgive you."

"Does God really care?"

"If you follow God and His ways you will be bored."

"If you go my way you will find fulfillment."

"God doesn't want you to have fun."

"What could be wrong with having a little fun?"

Just like in Genesis 3, the Devil makes promises that he can't fulfill. He promised Adam and Eve that they would be like God if they ate from the tree; and he promises you that you will gain freedom, fun, security, acceptance, and love if you give in to his temptations. But Satan's temptations are nothing more than mirages. He deceives us into believing that we can have a better reality than the one God has made for us.

(**"I GOT REALLY DRUNK ONE NIGHT AND HAD TWO GUYS TAKE ADVANTAGE OF ME."**)

TWO-FACED

In Revelation 12:10, after identifying Satan as the deceiver, John went on to say, "For the accuser of our brothers, who accuses them before our God day and night, has been hurled down." Satan isn't content just as deceiver; when he succeeds in tempting us, he shows another side of himself: *accuser.* In Hebrew the word *hasatan,* which actually means "accuser," is where we get our word *Satan.*

After you give in to temptation, Satan turns around and hammers on you for your sin. His barrage may sound something like this:

"How could you have done that?"

"I thought you were a Christian."

"How could you have been so stupid?"

"You are so horrible! You should be so ashamed of yourself."

"Your life is over. You have ruined it all. You're a joke."

He piles on embarrassment, disappointment, frustration, fear, guilt, and shame by the truckload. The smooth-sounding tone, pseudo-promises, and seductive words of the deceiver quickly morph into the soul-crushing, shame-laden, degrading words of the accuser. He sweet talks us into believing a lie and then accuses us of being terrible human beings for doing what he asked.

As soon as Adam and Eve gave in to the lies of the serpent, they looked for a hiding place. Why? They hid because shame had taken root in their hearts. Adam and Eve carried a burden that wasn't meant for them. Shame forces us to carry something we don't need to carry—but the enemy wants us to think that the burden is ours and that we deserve it.

("I CAN'T STOP ENGAGING IN CYBERSEX. I'M SO LONELY IT MAKES ME FEEL GOOD FOR A FEW MINUTES LIKE I'M USEFUL TO SOMEONE. I CAN'T GET AWAY FROM IT.")

After falling to temptation and realizing that they were naked, Adam and Eve hid. Shame causes us to hide and run from God. Hiding produces the perfect environment for shame to grow, because shame flourishes in the dark.

REPEAT

Convincing you to believe a lie and carry shame is really just the beginning of Satan's strategy. However, the plan doesn't get increasingly complex; rather he just repeats the first two steps.

Satan continues his onslaught, turning into the deceiver once again, trying to convince you of new possibilities. The deception is the same, but this time he takes advantage of your guilt and shame, saying things like:

"You are feeling so terrible about yourself and need some comfort. Try this."

"This will make everything better."

"You already blew it once, you might as well do it again. This time it will deliver."

If we respond to his lies again, the enemy transforms again from *deceiver* to *accuser*:

"I can't believe you did that again."

"Didn't you learn your lesson the first time? How stupid are you?"

"You are pathetic."

The accusations shift from strong declarations against *what you did* to attack *who you are.* "I did something bad" morphs into "I am bad."

The goal of this attack is to turn guilt and shame into despair. You didn't just cheat; you are a cheater. You didn't just do a perverted thing; you are a pervert. This is what you do and who you are. You are hopeless and will never be anything else.

> "I DON'T KNOW IF ANY OTHER GIRL STRUGGLES WITH MASTURBATION. I CAN'T STOP. I'LL GO MONTHS WITHOUT DOING IT AND THEN IT JUST TAKES ME OVER."

The cycle repeats again and again until helplessness sets in. We try to turn to God and dedicate our lives to His service, but after numerous failures, our dedications become rededications. Soon we become completely immersed in the enemy's lies.

The enemy's hook is fully set when we make the connection between what we do and who we are in our hearts. After several rounds of deceiver/accuser, deceiver/accuser, the final deceit often sounds something like this:

"I don't even know how you can call yourself a Christian anymore."

"You should just forget this God thing."

"Actually He doesn't want anything to do with you."

Satan wants us to believe that God will reject us if we run to Him, convincing us that we had better run away from Him. Satan blinds us to God's compassion and mercy and skews our perception of God. Convinced that God is mad at us, we buy into the lie that He will destroy us instead of the truth that God welcomes us in any state. Satan also knows that the best way to keep you from running to God is to keep you away from others, *living in isolation.*

"You need to forget your Christian community."

"You aren't good enough for them."

> **"I GET JEALOUS OF EVERY SKINNY GIRL I SEE."**

"Dodge your accountability group, skip your small group, avoid church—they really don't want you around anyway."

Ultimately Satan's lies separate us from God.

EXCHANGE

The jumbotron sign reads: "TRAP AHEAD. DECEIVE, ACCUSE. REPEAT."

So how do we avoid the cycle or get out of it if it's already spinning?

Though the pattern is simple, it isn't always obvious like a jumbotron message. Often the message is subtle enough to escape notice but still strong enough to influence our actions, attitudes, and beliefs.

(
    "I THINK THAT EVERYONE IS INFERIOR TO ME."
)

To begin with, we must believe that there is a way out. First Corinthians 10:13 says, "No temptation has seized you except what is common to man. And God is faithful; he will not let you be tempted beyond what you can bear. But when you are tempted, he will also provide a way out so that you can stand up under it."

No matter how stuck we feel, how far we've fallen, or how deep the mess—there is always a way out. The road might not be easy or short, but there is a way out! When Adam and Eve gave in to temptation, they believed the lie that God isn't good. They believed that what God had for them wasn't enough and accepted a lie as a truth.

Lies get us into this trap, but the truth gets us out. What lies do you believe as truth?

When you recognize the lie being pitched your way, you can counter it with the truth. We often fall to temptation and believe lies because we aren't armed with truth, only with our feelings. Our feelings lead us astray because they focus on the short-term. Because truth comes from God, it gives us an eternal perspective.

(**"I'M ADDICTED TO PRESCRIPTION PAIN KILLERS."**)

I love reading and praying through the Psalms. David expressed with direct and sometimes uncomfortable honesty his feelings and the lies he was tempted to believe. However, David always landed in truth. Look at Psalm 13 and notice how David started and how he ended this passage:

> How long, O LORD? Will you forget me forever?
>> How long will you hide your face from me?
> How long must I wrestle with my thoughts
>> and every day have sorrow in my heart?
>> How long will my enemy triumph over me?
> Look on me and answer, O LORD my God.
>> Give light to my eyes, or I will sleep in death;
> my enemy will say, "I have overcome him,"
>> and my foes will rejoice when I fall.
> But I trust in your unfailing love;
>> my heart rejoices in your salvation.
> I will sing to the LORD,
>> for he has been good to me.

After identifying the enemy's lie, search for the truth he is hiding from you. For example, if the deceiver feeds you the line "You need acceptance and will find it by sleeping with your boyfriend," you can counter that lie by praying:

"I feel the desire to give myself away and I realize that I want to be loved, but this I know to be true: *I am completely accepted by God.* The God of the universe has chosen me (Col. 3:12), and the love that God has for His Son, Jesus, is the same love He has for me (John 17:23). Lord, I am not going to believe the lie that I will find acceptance by violating Your ways."

The enemy tries to lead you into sin by first getting you to buy into his lies. However, if you address his lies with the Word of God, they lose power. In many ways this example is much less about the temptation to have sex than it is about the temptation to believe the lie that you are not already accepted and loved.

(**"I FEAR MY LIFE WILL AMOUNT TO NOTHING."**)

COMMUNITY

A couple of years ago I went on a safari in the Ngorongoro Crater in Tanzania, Africa. It was more spectacular than I could have imagined! As we drove around in open-topped safari vehicles looking for animals, we saw zebras, flamingos, and elephants everywhere. As beautiful as these animals were, everyone wanted to see a lion. A few hours later our driver received a radio tip, and we headed to a location where a few napping lions had been spotted earlier in the day. When we got there, our driver found a good place for us to get a good view and take pictures.

As we stared at the majestic king of beasts, the guide told us that when lions hunt, the isolated or weak animals are always the ones to get eaten. The lions wait in the grass on the outskirts of a herd of zebras or gazelles, waiting for one to wander away from the group. That wanderer gets targeted and soon becomes the lions' dinner.

(**"I STILL CAN'T FORGIVE MY FATHER FOR NOT BEING THERE FOR ME."**)

The evil one is the same with us. He waits for us to wander away from the strength found in the community of faith. He knows that when we're alone we can't draw on the protection that comes from being part of the body of Christ.

God made us for more than a life of individuality and isolation. He designed us to need each other and to gain strength from one another. We need community. We weren't meant to be lone rangers, destined to take the world on by ourselves. We are at our best and safest when we're connected with others. This is so eloquently stated in Ecclesiastes 4:9–12:

> It's better to have a partner than go it alone.
> Share the work, share the wealth.

And if one falls down, the other helps,

But if there's no one to help, tough!

Two in a bed warm each other.

Alone, you shiver all night.

By yourself you're unprotected.

With a friend you can face the worst.

Can you round up a third?

A three-stranded rope isn't easily snapped. (MSG)

ONE STEP

The difference between being eaten and staying alive on the African safari is *one step*. One step farther away from the pack than anyone else … one step slower than the lion. If we realize that we're all a single step away from disaster, we'll do whatever we can to stay in the middle of the pack.

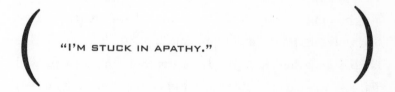

("I'M STUCK IN APATHY.")

I have many people in my life who help me stay close to the pack and out of the sights of the prowling enemy who would love to catch me napping (1 Peter 5:8 MSG). I don't have a formal accountability group that meets regularly, but I do have trusted friends who keep me from getting lazy, prideful, or isolated. I recognize that we're all one step from stupid, so I consider them my "one-step group." The way that I've found this to be most helpful is to tell them specifically and directly that they have full access to my life and permission to confront me on any issue. They will ask pointed questions, but because I know that we could easily miss each other, I also regularly ask them if they see anything in my life. These conversations are not always comfortable, but they help me identify the ways I might buy into lies, embrace accusations, or drive toward isolation.

For years now my close friends have acted as mirrors for the areas of my life that are regular temptations or blind spots. I've never enjoyed the initial pain of hearing how I've been arrogant, harsh, or unforgiving, but I keep in mind that these friends aren't trying to hurt me, they're only trying to help me. Proverbs 27:6 highlights the value of the sting of these words from those who are willing to confront me when it says, "Wounds from a friend can be trusted."

You may have your own accountability group (or want to begin one) or a one-step group. Whatever you call the group, I suggest that you make this kind of community a priority in your life. The key is to keep close those friends you can trust, who know you and will love you enough to confront you and be honest. Without a community like that, you are vulnerable, weak, and potential food for the enemy.

(   )

"I AM A GOSSIP."

Fully Satisfied

Don't look at page 193. And definitely don't look at the secret on that page!

I mean it; you shouldn't look at that page. Don't even glance at it. After you read page 192, skip straight to page 194. Whatever you do, don't look at page 193!

Were you tempted to look at page 193? Why? When we focus on something, especially something we're trying to avoid, the draw is incredibly powerful.

("SOMEONE I LOVE TOLD ME INTIMATE, DES-
PERATELY PRIVATE SECRETS ABOUT HIS LIFE
AND I TOLD ALL KINDS OF PEOPLE.")

I love Mountain Dew—original Mountain Dew specifically. New flavors have come out periodically over the years: LiveWire, Code Red, and most recently White Out. Sometimes I try them, but they aren't that tempting to me, and I don't care if they ever come out with another flavor. I have found that there is nothing like original Mountain Dew—to me, it is the nectar of heaven. It is the perfect blend of carbonated water and flavor. I am 100 percent confident I will not be tempted to embrace a new soda. Why? Because I have the best thing there is!

The biggest key to avoiding the traps of the enemy is to embrace the man who is Truth: *Jesus.* When we taste and see that the Lord is good, all other tastes pale in comparison.

J. I. Packer wrote, "While my fellow believers are constantly seeking to advance themselves in godliness, they show little direct interest in God himself."[29] Godliness without God is mere moralism and won't last. Our goal is to arrive at a place in which we become so satisfied by God that we enjoy living in obedience and truth more than we do sin.

In his raw and honest book *The Confessions*, fourth-century bishop and theologian Saint Augustine wrote of his struggle with lust. He was tormented by his belief in the lie that giving in to the temptation of lust was the greatest pleasure. Notice what he wrote when he finally experienced freedom:

> How sweet all at once it was for me to be rid of those fruitless joys which I had once feared to lose and was now glad to reject! You drove them from me, you who are the true, the sovereign joy. You drove them from me and took their place, you who are sweeter than all pleasure.[30]

The greatest defense against darkness is light. Where there is light, darkness is no more (1 John 1:5). So rather than focusing on the sin and the enemy, I've found that when I place my energy and focus on Jesus, the Light of the World, all the darkness fades.

REFLECTION

/// What lie has the enemy tempted you to believe as truth?

/// How has the Devil accused you in an attempt to isolate
you?

/// Do you have a community of people to protect you from
wandering off?

11

THE RIGHT SECRETS

We've spent a lot of time talking about secrets—ridding our hearts of them and living secret-free lives. What a great picture. Close your eyes and imagine this life of freedom. A life without secrets! Never sneaking around, and instead, experiencing the strength of a community of faith, walking in the light, and being fully known by others—this is how God wants us to live. Well, I have some news for you: Some secrets we're supposed to keep.

Before you think that I've gone crazy here, let me explain. Jesus encourages us to keep the right secrets—secrets that actually produce life.

Secret Santa

A few years ago I heard a pastor talking about a single mom who had recently sold her car to pay her bills. Her husband had abandoned her and her three children, leaving them with nothing. She went to school, worked a part-time job, rode the bus, and got rides from friends to get her kids to school. It was Christmastime, but gifts for her kids were out of the question. The bigger concern was if they were going to have a place to live next month or food on the table. She was on the edge of a cliff and about to fall off.

I immediately wondered if I could do anything. Then it hit me: I could help change everything for her! I called one of my staff members, gave her my credit card, and told her to go buy a car. Within 24 hours I was the owner of a Toyota Corolla with only 36,000 miles on it. It was a perfect, reliable car for a single mom. Now the problem was that I didn't have the money to pay off my credit card at the end of the month, but I had a plan. I meet with 1,000 college students every Friday night at theMILL; surely they would help me out.

But college students have no money, right? I know they might be poor, but I frequently see them drinking $4 drinks at Starbucks or eating $6 burritos. So I figured that all I had to do was get the students to give up a couple of drinks or burritos a month and we could give this family a new lease on life.

> "I'M USING THE MORTGAGE MONEY TO BUY A CAR BECAUSE I NEVER SAVED THE MONEY LIKE I WAS SUPPOSED TO. MY HUSBAND DOESN'T KNOW."

I told the students about the single mom, the car I bought, and how I wanted them to help out. I wanted us to pay for the car and the registration and give it to her later that week. I was extremely nervous, wondering if I had gotten myself into a bind. After the offering at theMILL that night, I was eager to find out what had been given. At the end of the night the total given was $30,000!

The next week we paid for the car and the registration and gave her a large gift card to Wal-Mart so she could fill her pantry and buy some gifts for her kids. Through this experience, we even found other single moms and blessed them with unexpected gifts as well.

(**"I DON'T KNOW IF I BELIEVE IN GOD."**)

Here's the beauty of this story: When we bought the car, I'd never even met this woman! And she had no idea that this was happening; she hadn't asked for anything. I called her to see if she could drop by the church to "pick something up." She later told me she thought we were going to give her a fruit basket. *What a surprise!* In a flash a major burden was lifted, and she was able to spend her time helping her kids with homework, and doing her own, instead of coordinating rides and fretting over bills.

See, this is what Jesus was talking about when He said:

> Be careful not to do your "acts of righteousness" before men, to be seen by them. If you do, you will have no reward from your Father in heaven.
>
> So when you give to the needy, do not announce it with trumpets, as the hypocrites do in the synagogues and on the streets, to be honored by men. I tell you the truth, they have received their

reward in full. But when you give to the needy, do
not let your left hand know what your right hand
is doing, so that your giving may be in secret. Then
your Father, who sees what is done in secret, will
reward you. (Matt. 6:1–4)

Since then we've made secret giving a common practice, not
only for theMILL but also for my family. My wife and I love
it when we hear about someone with a need that we can meet
anonymously. Money to fix a broken car, money for a mission
trip, money for gas, money for a trip home, or money to sponsor
a child living in poverty—it's like being a secret Santa all year
long!

The group gift from theMILL was unique, and though it got
some publicity, my favorite gifts are those that remain anonymous.
When the gift is truly a secret, it's quiet and unobtrusive and there
are no announcements.

What if the secrets in your heart were the gifts you'd given people
anonymously or the kingdom projects around the world in which
you'd invested? The size of the gift doesn't matter. Even if it's a large
gift, no plaque, fanfare, or public announcement is necessary. Why
not work on your undercover giving skills?

("EVEN THOUGH I'VE NEVER BEEN SEEN
WITHOUT A SMILE AND I SEEM TO HAVE
IT ALL TOGETHER, I'M BREAKING INSIDE.
SCARED OF LETTING EVERYONE DOWN
BECAUSE I'M NOT PERFECT.")

Go to Your Room

I sometimes wonder how often we dismiss teachings from the Bible because the culture or circumstance is different from our own. Take the story of Ananias and Sapphira in Acts 5, for instance: They sold land and didn't give all the profits to the apostles; and as a result of their deceit, they suddenly fell to the ground dead. So do we think, *Well, I haven't sold land and kept the proceeds from God, so this story doesn't apply to me?* Before we skip stories like this, it's important to recognize that there are greater lessons of integrity, obedience, and community in this story. Do we do this same thing when we read Matthew 6:5?

> And when you pray, do not be like the hypocrites,
> for they love to pray standing in the synagogues
> and on the street corners to be seen by men. I tell
> you the truth, they have received their reward in
> full.

Our quick response might be, *Well, I don't pray on street corners. I don't even pray in public, so I'm not the hypocrite that Jesus addresses here.*

"I LIE TO GET WHAT I WANT."

On one level, Jesus addresses an issue specific to that time and place. The Pharisees really did stand on the street praying aloud to garner attention and praise for themselves. However, at a deeper and more universal level, I believe that Jesus is most concerned with the condition of our hearts as we come to Him in prayer. Beyond that, Jesus is also encouraging us to develop secret lives of prayer.

Consider the very next verse:

> But when you pray, go into your room, close the
> door and pray to your Father, who is unseen. Then
> your Father, who sees what is done in secret, will
> reward you. (Matt. 6:6)

This is about protecting our hearts from seeking too much attention or praise for acts of worship, but it's also an exhortation to develop inner lives that aren't seen by others.

Jesus encourages us to create places where we can meet God without anyone listening, without anyone cheering us on, and without any agreements, accolades, or ulterior motives … *just us and God.*

What if it was your goal to keep your prayer life hidden and unnoticed? Would it look different? Would you choose a different location? Would you stop telling others that you spent time with God? I believe that prayers done in secret actually develop greater intimacy with God. As you become less distracted and more focused on the One, you will find that secret time with Him is reward enough. I like to think of this as a challenge to have a *stealth prayer life.* I don't make a big deal of when or how often I pray, but I do try to sneak away to a secret place.

(**"I BLAME MYSELF THAT MY DAD LEFT ME AND DOESN'T WANT ANYTHING TO DO WITH ME."**)

PLEASURE

Misery loves company.

When we face misery in our lives, we want people to share in our pain or know that we're suffering. This is true of many circumstances in life, but Jesus exhorts His followers to push this desire aside, specifically when it comes to *fasting:*

> When you fast, do not look somber as the hypocrites do, for they disfigure their faces to show men they are fasting. I tell you the truth, they have received their reward in full. But when you fast, put oil on your head and wash your face, so that it will not be obvious to men that you are fasting, but only to your Father, who is unseen; and your Father, who sees what is done in secret, will reward you. (Matt. 6:16–18)

The Pharisees fasted two days every week and made it their practice to look like they were dying of starvation, letting the world know that they were relinquishing earthly pleasures for more holy activities.

Of all the ways Jesus calls us to a secret life with Him, fasting is the most difficult for me. First, because I love food! My friends and I say that every conversation is better if food is included. I don't know if this is how it happens to you, but whenever I fast, without fail, I always see offers for free food or get invitations to free steak dinners. It's like there's a conspiracy to get me to stop fasting. I'm just trying to mind my own business and develop a secret life—*can't everyone cooperate?*

Second, fasting is hard. It's no fun to go without food for a single meal, let alone for a couple of days. When I fast, I usually feel like I'm experiencing my last days. I am dying a slow and horrible death. My stomach growls, I get headaches, I feel extremely tired, I can't concentrate on anything besides the time of my next meal, and time seems to stand still. I understand why the Pharisees looked the way they did … I certainly feel that way!

Rather than giving up or making a scene, I've learned to see these distractions as opportunities to develop my hidden life. So when someone says, "Aaron, let's go get Chipotle burritos for lunch—*I'm buying*," and everything in me screams, *Yes, I would love to, actually* I need to, *my stomach is eating itself right now because I'm so hungry*, instead I say, "No thanks."

I don't always succeed. But I do learn something through this experience. To forsake earthly pleasures—food or otherwise—tells me how important personal pleasures are in my life. Fasting reveals what controls me and reminds me of He who sustains me.

Am I controlled by my stomach? Am I sustained by God? Am I driven by what I want? Do I care what others think, or am I content to keep my fasting a secret? Is the reward of the Father enough for me, or do I need something else?

These are the questions Jesus presses on me as He encourages me to make fasting a covert operation.

HABITS

For the last few years my wife and I have taught our boys how to take care of their teeth by brushing on a daily basis. We began the process by showing them how to brush their teeth. Next, we brushed their teeth for them, which morphed into letting them brush their own teeth, with my wife and I finishing what they missed. Learning to rinse and spit was always a big milestone, after which we arrived at the place where they could do it all on their own. Even though they know how to brush their teeth now, we still have to remind them to brush before they go to bed and when they get up in the morning. Of course the goal is that they will take care of their teeth without being reminded.

(
**"I ONLY PRETEND TO LIKE HALF MY FRIENDS.
I REALLY CAN'T STAND THEM."**
)

This daily routine is intended to cultivate a habit. Similarly it requires repetition and routine to cultivate spiritual habits that will develop virtue. Author, leading theologian, and bishop of Durham for the Church of England N. T. Wright wrote about this in his book *After You Believe*:

> Virtue ... is what happens when someone has made a thousand small choices, requiring effort and concentration, to do something which is good and right but which doesn't "come naturally"—and then, on the thousand and first time, when it really

matters, they find that they do what's required
"automatically," as we say. On that thousand and
first occasion, it does indeed look as if it "just happens"; but reflection tells us it doesn't "just happen"
as easily as that.[31]

Virtue doesn't just come by accident. It comes through the self-
discipline required to do anything in life really well.

We will never know how many cavities we avoided through our
vigorous brushing routine, but we know it is important. This good
habit can protect us from mouthfuls of pain. Living in the light and
developing an inner life of giving, prayer, and fasting can often feel
the same way. These habits protect us from the unknown. We may
never know precisely what sin we've avoided, but the continual practice of these disciplines is immeasurably valuable.

(**"I STILL MAKE MYSELF THROW UP. EVEN
THOUGH I TOLD EVERYONE I STOPPED."**)

Notice in the Matthew 6 passage that in all three disciplines
Jesus didn't say *if,* He said *when.* These were things His followers
would do. Just like brushing teeth isn't an option at the Stern house,
giving, prayer, and fasting is something we *will* do. Jesus goes so
much deeper than the basic practices. He gets at our hearts.

There is something about being heart focused that frees us, and
that's why Jesus continually addresses the heart. He lambasted the

Pharisees for neglecting the heart, pointed the rich ruler toward an issue of the heart, and praised the widow for her fully devoted heart (Matt. 23; Luke 18; Mark 12). When we're convicted of greed, it's not about money; when we lust, it's not about sex; and when we get angry, it's not about revenge—it's all about what happens in the secret places of our hearts.

(**"I'M PLAYING CHURCH."**)

Oswald Chambers, the author of *My Utmost for His Highest*, once said, "The secret of religion is religion in secret."

What if we spent as much energy on developing this hidden spiritual life as we have keeping soul-destroying secrets?

REWARDS

We all love rewards. It's built into our nature. My boys clean up their room for a sticker on a sheet that tracks good behavior, my wife gives herself a chocolate as a treat after a long day, and I mow the lawn for personal satisfaction and the admiration of neighbors. We all love to receive praise after a job well done. It's not a problem that we like rewards—we were designed to love rewards—but an issue arises when we become accustomed to and addicted to immediate gratification.

We want our rewards now!

When Jesus talked about giving, prayer, and fasting, He said that if we don't do them in secret then we will have already received our rewards, which are immediate and short-term in that case. As we read the Sermon on the Mount, Jesus followed His encouragements for a secret life by saying:

> Do not store up for yourselves treasures on earth, where moth and rust destroy, and where thieves break in and steal. But store up for yourselves treasures in heaven, where moth and rust do not destroy, and where thieves do not break in and steal. For where your treasure is, there your heart will be also. (Matt. 6:19–21)

Jesus exhorted us to keep a long-term perspective and patiently wait to receive our rewards *later*. He said that earthly treasure—the admiration and recognition of others—is not only short-lived but also ultimately worthless. However, keeping an eternal perspective will pay dividends in the kingdom of God. It's about seeing physical treasures as less valuable than spiritual treasure.

("I HAD SEX EXACTLY ONE WEEK BEFORE MY WEDDING, WHEN I HAD WAITED MY WHOLE LIFE.")

What if we really believed what Jesus said? Would we look for opportunities to give, pray, and fast in secret in order to accumulate heavenly treasure? Would we keep things hidden and gain the attention of the One?

The Conclusion of the Matter

Maybe the thought of developing a positive secret life excites you and you've already scheduled a time to fast next week. Or perhaps you feel overwhelmed and think, *I've barely managed to confess my secrets to God, and I'm still trying to work up the courage to talk to somebody else about them.*

("I COULD HAVE THREE CHILDREN ... I'M 21.")

Wherever you're at today, I encourage you to move forward. Review the chapters in this book and identify your next step. The important thing to remember is that this is a journey. Whether you stand at the beginning, the middle, or the end is of no consequence. God calls us away from darkness and into the light. He calls us out of lives of burden and shame and into lives of freedom and hope. If you realize that you have secrets eating you from the inside out, *confess them to God.* If you've never confessed to the person you've sinned against, call that person up today. If you can make restitution, begin by determining what is necessary and possible. If you find yourself stuck in a cycle where freedom is tasted but not lived, identify baggage that can be unpacked, forgiveness that can be offered, or lies that can be exchanged for truth. Finally, if you're living for short-term rewards, develop the secret habits necessary to build up your long-term, heavenly rewards.

For those of you who have buried your secrets deep or are dealing with some heavy baggage, beginning this journey may seem impossible. There's probably a part of you that wants a guarantee—you want to know that the risk of sharing your secrets will be worth it. You want to know how this journey will look, step-by-step, and how it will end. Well, God doesn't usually work that way. As I've said from the beginning, this isn't a ten-step program. Ultimately you must lean on God. And while He doesn't often point out the exact route on a map, He does something better. He walks with you and promises never to leave your side.

It's been over four years since I preached the sermon series that resulted in this book, and I can't tell you how many different paths this journey can take.

Some have found and cultivated stronger community, others have made the switch from being transparent to vulnerable, others have enlisted the help of a professional baggage unpacker, while others have wrestled through their personal value as a result of what someone else did to them. Some changes have been easy while other changes have been hard; some changes were obvious while others were subtler.

The common theme for each person I've seen walk this journey is this: Exchanging secrets of sin and shame for a secret life with God is powerful, life changing, and worthwhile.

God is calling, the journey is waiting, and freedom is possible.

REFLECTION

/// What can you do to grow as a giver?

/// How can you develop a secret prayer life?

/// What can you do to cultivate a lifestyle of fasting from various things in your life?

ACKNOWLEDGMENTS

Gratefulness fills my heart as I consider the people who have impacted my life to make this book a reality. If it weren't for these influences and their encouragements, I'm pretty sure this book would never have been started or at best be a half-finished manuscript with only good intentions to finish it. This book is only possible because of you. Thank you.

Mom: Your many years of prayer taught me that what we don't see is more than we know.

Dad: Despite all my complaining during the years of waking up early, cleaning up job sites, and pulling nails, you never once threatened to fire me! You taught me how to work hard, finish what I start, and do all things well.

theMILL: This book happened because of you. Your willingness to engage the process of freedom and walk out truth turned into something bigger than a monthlong series. Thank you for allowing me the privilege to be your pastor. It is an honor to journey with you.

theMILL staff: Thank you for leading this community with me.

Glenn Packiam, Rob Brendle, David Perkins: You demonstrate the strength and sharpening found in true friendship. I would walk through anything with you.

Noelle Goodlin and Sarabeth Harrelson: Thank you for carving out the time to work with the very rough drafts. Your feedback was invaluable to my process as a writer.

Don Pape: It was in the booth at Ted's Montana Grill that I realized this was more than just a nice idea but could actually become a reality. Thank you for trusting me.

Alex Field and the Cook team: Passive verbs and tense changes are no more because of you. Your editing prowess made this book better.

Parker, Cohen, Brooks, and Smith: I love being your dad.

Jossie: Thank you for giving me time to write, listening to me read, and believing in me before anyone else did. I love my life with you!

Jesus: You are my greatest joy. Thank You for freedom.

NOTES

1. Michael Castleman, "Marital Infidelity: How Common Is It?" *Psychology Today*, www.psychologytoday.com/blog/all-about-sex/200910/marital-infidelity-how-common-is-it (accessed April 14, 2011).

2. Don Colbert, *Deadly Emotions* (Nashville, TN: Thomas Nelson, 2006).

3. Eugene Peterson, *The Jesus Way* (Grand Rapids, MI: Eerdmans, 2007), 91–92.

4. Neil T. Anderson, *Victory Over the Darkness* (Ventura, CA: Regal, 2000), 228.

5. Peterson, *The Jesus Way*, 92.

6. Frederick Buechner, *Telling Secrets* (New York: HarperCollins, 1991), 3.

7. Frank Warren, *PostSecret* (New York: William Morrow, 2005), 116.

8. Buechner, *Telling Secrets*, 39.

9. Jeff Cook, *Seven* (Grand Rapids, MI: Zondervan, 2008), 46.

10. F. Scott Fitzgerald, *The Great Gatsby* (Sioux Falls, SD: NuVision, 2008), 7.

11. Thomas Brooks, *A Cabinet of Choice Jewels* in *The Complete Works of Thomas Brooks*, vol. 3 (Edinburgh, UK: James Nichol, 1669), 405.

12. Jim Forest, *Confession* (Maryknoll, NY: Orbis, 2002).

13. Tertullian, as quoted in James Dallen, *The Reconciling Community* (New York: Pueblo, 1986), 33.

14. Justo L. González, *The Story of Christianity*, vol. 1 (New York: HarperCollins, 2010), 288.

15. John Henry Hopkins, *The History of the Confessional* (New York: Harper & Brothers, 1850), 14.

16. "Syllabus Condemning the Errors of the Modernists," Papal Encyclicals Online, www.papalencyclicals.net/Pius10/p10lamen.htm (accessed March 24, 2011), pars. 49–50.

17. *Book of Common Prayer* (Kingsport, TN: Kingsport, 1977), 320.

18. Father Thomas Richstatter, "Ten Tips for Better Confessions," American Catholic, www.americancatholic.org/Newsletters/CU/ac0890.asp (accessed January 27, 2011), pars. 8–11.

19. Dietrich Bonhoeffer, *The Cost of Discipleship* (New York: Touchstone, 1995), 44–45.

20. Richard J. Foster, *Celebration of Discipline,* 3rd ed. (New York: HarperCollins, 1998), 145–46.

21. Buechner, *Telling Secrets,* 2–3.

22. A. W. Tozer, *The Pursuit of Man* (Camp Hill, PA: Christian Publications, 1950), 19–20.

23. I owe this definition to Louie Giglio, founder of Passion Conferences and pastor of Passion City Church in Atlanta, Georgia.

24. Eugene Peterson, *Practice Resurrection* (Grand Rapids, MI: Eerdmans, 2010), 68.

25. Ibid., 252.

26. N. T. Wright, *After You Believe* (New York: HarperOne, 2010), 24.

27. Timothy Keller, *The Prodigal God* (New York: Penguin, 2008), 55.

28. Miroslav Volf, *Exclusion and Embrace* (Nashville, TN: Abingdon, 1994).

29. J. I. Packer, *Meeting God* (Downers Grove, IL: InterVarsity, 2001), 5.

30. Saint Augustine, *The Confessions; The City of God; On Christian Doctrine* (Chicago: Encyclopædia Britannica, 1990), 78.

31. Wright, *After You Believe,* 20–21.